TAX DEDUCTION & COLLECTION AT SOURCE

Issues, Judgements and Clarifications

VED KUMAR JAIN

MANOHAR
2004

First published 2004

ISBN 81-7304-546-1

Published by
Ajay Kumar Jain for
Manohar Publishers & Distributors
4753/23 Ansari Road, Daryaganj
New Delhi 110 002

Printed at
Lordson Publishers Pvt. Ltd.
Delhi 110 007

CONTENTS

FOREWORD

Keeping in touch with the latest developments is part of the essential equipment in our profession as it is in any other. This is particularly so in these fast-changing times. We need to have a reliable, easy-to-consult compendium of information that is succinct and is lucidly written and that we can reach out to as we sit on our working desk. In this context this monograph on Tax Deduction and Collection at Source by Ved Kumar Jain is most welcome. It deals with an important subject in the area of income taxation and presents the issues and judgements and clarifications connected with it with competence and clarity.

Ved Kumar Jain is an eminent member of the fraternity of chartered accountants, who has distinguished himself in various fields. He is a popular speaker and is invited to address seminar and conferences across the country. His wide and varied experience, his clarity on tax issues, his objectivity and his interaction with fellow professionals make him eminently fit to write on the subject.

I have no doubt that fellow chartered accountants will find it a useful reference book to have on their desk.

N.D. GUPTA
Past President
The Institute of Chartered Accountants of India

New Delhi

PREFACE

Tax deduction at source, commonly known as TDS is an area that has become increasingly complex over the years. The person obliged to deduct tax, often find it difficult to comply with its many requirements despite the best of intention. Equally, Professional colleagues do find it no easier to answer the various queries. In the course of my interaction with colleagues at seminars and conferences, I have felt the need for compendium of information on different aspects of tax deduction and collection at source.

Keeping these difficulties in view, I have tried to put all essential uptodate information relating to this aspect of taxation in a easy-to-consult book that could serve as a reference tool.

An effort has been made to deal with all the issues involved in the area of tax deduction and collection and suggest how procedures could be simplified and rationalized. Important official circulars, clarifications and summaries of relevant judgments have been reproduced. Three appendices at the end give current data relating to rate of tax deduction at source, date schedule for deposit of tax and tax rates as per double taxation avoidances agreement with different countries.

I hope the book will serve the purpose of placing all the relevant and latest information about tax deduction at source within easy reach of the professionals.

New Delhi

VED KUMAR JAIN

1. ISSUES ON TAX DEDUCTION AT SOURCE

Introduction

Tax deduction at source has become the most effective tool of collection of tax with the government. The objective of introducing tax deduction at source, commonly known as withholding tax across the world, was to reduce the hardship of tax payers in filing return of income individually and to get their tax paid through the person responsible of making payment of the income. But over the period, the scope of these provisions are being widened to have better compliance and collect tax from those persons, whom the tax authorities have failed to get hold of. But in the process, the obligation on the tax deductor has increased considerably. Normally, it is the responsibility of the person who earns the income to pay tax thereon, but under these provisions, the duty to deduct and pay tax, is shifted to the person making payment of such income. At the time of introduction of the Income Tax Act, 1961 these provisions were applicable to only 4 categories of payment namely on salaries under Section 192, on interest on securities under Section 193, on dividend under Section 194 and on payment to non residents under Section 195. But over the period, the scope has been widened and 23 types of payments as on date are covered by tax deduction at source provisions.

The objective of better compliance and avoidance of tax evasion is well conceived. But over the period the obligation and administrative work on the tax deductor has increased considerably and that too without any reward. The commission appointed way back in 1948 (Income Tax Investigation Commission) and the two commission in 1954 and 1958-1959 have not approved such provisions. It would have been ideal if the revenue in its zeal to collect more taxes and shifting its own responsibility of collecting tax through efficient administration, to tax deductor, had taken into consideration the valuable contribution being rendered by the deductor and consequently made the procedure of complying these provision simple, and more liberal rather than complicated and burdensome, which we have presently.

The provisions regarding TDS are contained in Section 190 to Section 206 and the rules dealing with the TDS are contained in rules 26 to 37A of the IT Rules. The forms which are required to be filled up by a person who is deducting and in turn depositing the tax at source are in Form No. 12B to Form No. 27A.

Procedure and Scheme of TDS

The obligation to deduct tax at source is upon "the person responsible for paying the income or an amount which is subject to TDS". Therefore, such person i.e. payer has to follow several procedures for deducting the tax from the hands of the recipient, who is really the person in receipt of income. In other words though it is the payee who has to pay the income-tax; procedure and liabilities under the scheme of TDS is on the payer. The main responsibilities and procedure of TDS are summarised as under:

(i) To apply for Tax Deduction Account No.

(ii) To deduct TDS from the income mentioned in the scheme at the prescribed rate.

(iii) To deposit such amount of TDS within stipulated time to the credit of Central Government.

(iv) To issue TDS certificate to the payees.

(v) To file various forms and returns as prescribed for having deducted and paid TDS.

<u>Issues</u>

(a) By and large on all payments liable for tax deduction, tax is to be deducted by "a person" as defined in Section 2(31) of the Act. But, individual and Hindu Undivided Family (HUF) other than those subjected to tax audit in the immediately preceding year are exempted by and large. However, TDS has to be deducted by all individual and HUF in case of payments made for salary under Section 192, payment of commission on lottery tickets, under Section 194 G payments for lottery under Section 194B.

(b) Every person deducting tax in accordance with the provisions of this Act is required to obtain tax deduction account number (TAN). It can be Individual, Hindu undivided family, Society, Trust, Firm or a Company, etc. The application for TAN is to be made in Form No. 49B in duplicate to the authority having jurisdiction assigned for this purpose. As provided in Section 206A, after its amendment by Finance Act, 1999, every person deducting tax in accordance with the provisions of Sections under this Chapter, if he has not been allotted any TAN, shall, within the prescribed time (within one month from the end of the month in which tax is deducted at source) apply to the Assessing Officer (jurisdiction authority) for allotment of TAN. Once the TAN is allotted to the person, such person is required to quote such number:

(i) in all challans for the payment of any sum in accordance with the provisions of Section 200;

(ii) in all certificates issued in accordance with the provisions of Section 203;

(iii) in all the returns delivered in accordance with the provisions of Section 206, 206A and 206B, to any income-tax authority, and

(iv) in all other documents pertaining to such transactions as may be prescribed in the interest of revenue.

(c) If a person fails to comply with the requirement i.e. if he does not apply in Form No. 49B within the prescribed time, or after allotment fails to quote such TAN in the challan, certificate, returns then he is liable to a penalty under Section 272BB. Such penalty can be levied by the Assessing Officer or by the TDS Officer, which is maximum up to Rs. 10,000. The order for levying penalty is 'however' appealable.

(d) Separate number has to be obtained to meet the requirement of Section 206C. i.e. Tax Collection at Source (TCAN)

(e) Every payer (other than Government) is required to pay the tax deducted at source to the Government within the prescribed time and in the prescribed manner.

1.3 TDS on Salaries%Section 192

(a) Liability of TDS

The liability to deduct tax at source is on all person whether individual, HUF, Firm or a company, irrespective of the fact whether the person is carrying on business or not. TDS on salaries is to be deducted in case a domestic servant or driver is being paid salary exceeding the maximum amount not chargeable to tax.

(i) The responsibility to deduct TDS is on the person who pays income chargeable under the head "Salaries". Therefore, the liability would arise only if the employer-employee relationship has been established. In other words, if work is done by a servant to the master on temporary basis or on contractual basis and if there is no relation of employer and employee, provisions of Section 192 will not be attracted

(ii) However, if recipient ceases to be an employee, but is paid by an employer for the services rendered in past, subsequent to the employee's resignation/ termination then provisions of TDS will be attracted for the salary paid by the employer to the erstwhile employee.

(iii) Therefore, payment made by the employer which is taxable under the Act as salary would attract TDS. Salary paid to non-resident Indians (NRI) rendering services in India is subject to TDS. But salaries paid to NRI for services rendered outside India will not be subject to TDS.

(b) Amount of TDS

(i) As provided in Section 192(1) tax is to be deducted at average rate of income–tax in force on estimated income. The word "estimated income" means employer has to make an honest estimate of the salary payable to the employee at the time of payment. So if there is a short deduction and the estimate is bona fide, the employer cannot be subject to interest or penalty.

(ii) The onus to prove estimate was bonafide is on the employer. Therefore, short TDS made due to increments given later on, calculation mistake, increment not considered, etc. can be considered as bona fide/honest estimate.

(iii) Various deductions can be considered while determining the estimate of salary by employer like 80CCE, 80D, 80DD, 80DDA, 80E, 80G (specified), 80GG and 80U. From 1st August, 1998, loss on account of property income can be considered by the employer. The employee at his option can submit statement of particulars of his other income along with a verification in the following form :-

Form of Verification

I, ... (name of the assessee), do declare that what is stated above is true to the best of my information and belief.

(Prescribed form 12C has been omitted with effect from 1st October, 2003.) Thereupon the employer is to take into consideration such other income while deducting tax. However loss, if any, other than the loss under the head income from house property has to be ignored. Therefore, if employee gives wrong information or details, the employer cannot be held liable for interest or penalty for non or short deduction of TDS. There is no penalty on employee for giving a calculation of deduction which is later on proved to be incorrect or excessive under wrong belief or impression.

(iv) Rebate available under Sections 88, 88B and 88C can be considered by the employer. Employer should obtain the proof of investment made by the employee and should not rely on simple declaration or oral assurance. However, employer cannot ask the employee to prove the source of investment *[See State Bank of Patiala vs. CIT & Anr. (1999) 236 ITR 281 (P&H)]*.

(v) Employees who are entitled to relief under Section 89(1) can furnish the information in the prescribed form to the employer, and in such cases employer can adjust the amount of TDS by allowing relief available under Section 89(i). *[See Sant Raj & Ors. vs. O.P. Singla & Ors. (1987) 163 ITR 588 (SC)*.

(vi) Leave encashment salary is exempt subject to limits and rules prescribed and TDS has to be made after considering such limits. However, encashment of leave salary paid to the legal heir after the death of the employee is not covered under s. 192. *[See CBDT Circular No. 309, dated 3rd July, 1981 [(1981) 25 CTR (TLT) 39]*

(vii) Amount paid by the employer to ex-employee on retrenchment by way of compensation is also not covered under Section 192. *[See Mahendra Singh*

Dhantwal vs. Hindustan Motors Ltd. (1985) 45 CTR (SC) 95: (1985) 152 ITR 68 (SC) : TC 5R.229].

(viii) Payments under Voluntary Retirement Scheme (VRS) are exempt under Section 10(10C).

(ix) Though payment received on superannuation is exempt under Section 10(13), the receipts from superannuation on premature retirement is not exempt after 1995. In such cases TDS provisions will be attracted.

(x) It is for the employer to prove the allowances and perquisites given to the employee are tax-free and not to be included in the salary. As the value of perquisites are to be computed by the employer while deducting tax, the value of the same is to be determined by the employer and not by the employee. This has to be done according to the Board's circular and case laws.

(c) Accrual of TDS

(i) TDS is deductible at the time of payment of salary and not on accrual of salary. Therefore, if the employee works but he is not paid then mere accrual does not make any liability to TDS. *[See Asstt. CIT vs. Smt. Shanti Devi Saraf (1994) 51 ITD 83 (Bom)].*

(ii) If an assessee is employed with more than one employer, he has an option to furnish the information of salary received from other employer. On submitting such information in Form No. 12B, the present employer has to deduct TDS of the earlier/other employer also. It is important to keep in mind that in such an event TDS not deducted by other employer in earlier period cannot be considered for interest or penalty.

(iii) The employer is entitled to increase or reduce the amount of TDS for any excess or deficiency. But such adjustment is permissible only in respect of same employee and not for all employees. Controversy normally arises when such variation is adjusted in last quarter or last month. Interest under Section 201(1A) is not leviable if exact amount of TDS is not deducted each month. *[See ITO vs. Asian Hotels Ltd. (1991) 41 TTJ (Del) 28 and Executive Engg. T.L.C. Division vs. ITO (1987) 28 TTJ (Hyd) 580].*

(iv) If after the year is over, there is a short TDS due to honest and bona fide belief by the employer and employee make good this shortfall in his return of income, the employer is not to recover such shortfall and he cannot be penalised. *[See CIT vs. Shri Synthetic Ltd. (1984) 39 CTR (MP) 72 : (1985) 151 ITR 634 (MP) : TC 5R.598 and also Gwalior Rayon Silk Co. Ltd. vs. CIT (1983) 37 CTR (MP) 351 : (1983) 140 ITR 832 (MP) : TC 5R.587].*

v) Employer is required to issue certificate in Form No.16 and a statement in Form No.12BA giving particulars of perquisites and value thereof if the amount of salary (as defined in rule 3) is more than Rs.1, 50,000.

vi) The rate of exchange on any income payable in foreign currency liable for TDS is the TT buying rate adopted by State Bank of India for such currency as on the date on which tax is required to be deducted at source.

vii) TDS return is to be filed in Form No.24, annually by 30th June, giving details of total amount chargeable under the head 'salaries' paid to all persons whose income for the year under the head salaries exceeded the maximum amount which is not taxable under the Finance Act of the year.

1.4 TDS on Interest on Securities–Section 193

(a) Liability of TDS

Consequent to omission of Sections 18 to 21 of the Income-tax Act with effect from 1st April, 1989 and insertion of Section 2(28B), which was inserted simultaneously, now "interest on security" means

(i) interest on any security of the Central Government or a State Government;

(ii) interest on debentures or other securities for money issued by or on behalf of a local authority or a company or a corporation established by a Central, State or Provincial Act;

(iii) As per amendment to proviso to Section 193 with effect from 1st June, 1997 and other amendments, interest payable on any security of the Central Government or a State Government is exempt from TDS with effect from 1st June, 1997. As per CBDT Circular No. 763 dated 18th February, 1998, this has been done to attract investment in Government securities.

(iv) Other than the above, all interest on securities is liable for deduction of TDS under Section 193 and the list of securities are stated in the Section. Accordingly, any person responsible for paying any income by way of income from securities must deduct tax at source and such person can be a firm, company, individual or corporation.

(v) The tax is to be deducted at the time of credit of such interest to the account of payee or at the time of payment thereof whichever is earlier. It is to be noted that except in case of Central or State Government, if a person merely credits the amount of interest and does not pay, because the payment is to be accumulated and to be paid later on even then he has to deduct the TDS and pay such amount to the Central Government.

(b) Amount of TDS

The amount of TDS is at the rate of income–tax in force on the amount of interest payable. Here, the payer works out the actual interest on the basis of the contract or promise as the case may be. No TDS however, is required to be deducted, if interest on debentures payable by a company to an individual does not exceed Rs. 2,500 in a financial year. This limit is of Rs. 10,000 in case of interest payable on certain gold bonds.

As provided in Section 197A(1A) if the recipient (other than a company or a firm) files a declaration in duplicate in Form 15G, no tax is required to be deducted.

(c) Procedure

The person responsible for deducting TDS has to issue a certificate of TDS in Form No. 16A within one month from the date for credit or payment. The payee has to file such certificate in original along with his income-tax return. The payer deducting the tax has to file annual return in Form No. 25 by 30th June every year. This form as amended from 19th March, 1997, is quite in detail and elaborate. The person, who has deducted the tax at the time of credit or payment, must deposit the tax within the prescribed time.

1.5 <u>TDS on Dividend–Section 194</u>

The income chargeable to tax under the head 'dividend' has been exempted again from 1st April, 2003. Therefore, provisions relating to TDS on dividend as envisaged under Section 194 are not applicable in respect of any dividends which is liable for distribution tax under Section 115-O of the Act..

(a) Liability of TDS

The liability of deduction of TDS is on the Principal Officer of an Indian company. Dividend is defined in Section 2(22). The exemption of non-deduction of TDS was available to a company paying dividend by an account payee cheque of an amount not exceeding Rs. 2,500.

(b) Amount of TDS

Till 31st May, 1997 the rate of TDS was 20 per cent. For dividend payable on or after 1st June, 1997 no tax was deductible. The controversial point is whether TDS is to be deducted if the recipient is taxed under Section 2(22)(e) by way of deemed dividend. As per a judgment of the Supreme Court, whenever the recipient is taxed under Section 2(22)(e) as deemed dividend; there is no liability of the company to deduct tax from whose accumulated profits, dividend is taxed in the hands of the shareholder, Punjab Distilling Industries Ltd. vs. CIT (1965) 57 ITR 1 (SC). But this judgment is under the old Act of 1922. The present Section 194 refers to dividend within the meaning of Section 2 (22) and includes sub-clauses (a) (b) (c) (d) and (e).

(c) Accrual of TDS

The tax is to be deducted at the time of payment of dividend. The tax so deducted under Section 194(1) by the Principal Officer is to be deposited to the credit of Central Government within 7 days of the deduction.

(d) Additional tax on dividend distributed under Section 115-O :

With effect from 1st April,2003, this provision has been re-inserted by which a company which pays the dividend out of current or accumulated profit shall be charged to additional income-tax at the rate of 12.5 percent. Thus over and above the normal tax of 35 percent, the company shall have to pay distribution tax if the dividend is declared, distributed or paid. Such tax on distributed profits is required to be paid within 14 days from the date of such declaration, distribution or payment, whichever is earliest.

It is further provided in Section 115-P that if a person fails to pay such additional tax within 14 days, then the company shall be liable to pay interest at the rate of 1.25 percent (reduced to 1.00 per cent per month with effect from 8.9.2003) for every month or part thereof of default.

It is important to note that no return on the lines of returns prescribed in Section 206 is prescribed for tax paid under Section 115-O. As such there is no check on the payment of such tax deducted and paid.

1.6 TDS on Interest–Section 194A

TDS is to be deducted on interest payment other than interest on securities. The term "interest" has been defined to mean interest payable in any manner in respect of monies borrowed or debt incurred including deposits, claim or other similar right or obligation. As defined in Section 2(28A), it also includes any service fee or any other charge in respect of the moneys borrowed or debt incurred or in respect of any credit facility, which has not been utilised. Thus, financial charges received under the guise of interest may also be covered under this provision. Charges like 'late payment penalty', 'cost of delayed recovery' etc. can be considered as interest or not is a debatable issue.

(a) Liability of TDS

Liability to deduct tax at source under this head is on every person other than an individual or HUF whose total sales, gross receipts or turnover from business or profession carried on by him does not exceed the limit prescribed under Section 44AB of the Act i.e. Rs.forty lacs in business or Rs.ten lac in profession in the immediate preceding financial year. Except the items which are specifically excluded under Section 194A (3), tax is to be deducted while paying or crediting the interest as explained above. The exclusion includes amount of such income where aggregate of such income credited or paid during the financial year does not exceed Rs.5000.

(b) Accrual of TDS

TDS has to be deducted at the time of credit of such interest to the account of the payee (or any other account by whatever name called in the books of accounts of the person paying interest) or at the time of payment whichever is earlier. The Section has provided various exemptions to certain Government corporations and institutions to which these provisions are not applicable. The tax deducted is to be deposited within one week from the last date of the month in which the deduction is made except when the same is credited on the day up to which accounts are made. In such case tax is to be deposited within 2 months from that date.

(c) Issues

(i) If there are deposits in the same branch of the bank in the name of a father and minor child, but the interest is less than Rs. 5,000 then no tax is deductible under Section 194A.Though under Section 64(1A) the interest income of minor is to be clubbed in the hands of father, for Section 194A such clubbing provision is not applicable.

(ii) The CBDT in Circular No. 715 dated 8th August, 1995 [(1995) 127 CTR (St) 13: (1995) 215 ITR 18 (St)] has clarified that tax has to be deducted at source at the time of credit or interest to the account of the payee or at the time of payment whichever is earlier. So even if credit is given not to the account of payee but to suspense account or interest payable account, even then the tax is to be deducted. Further it has been clarified by the Board that if the time deposits taken before 1st July, 1995, are renewed retrospectively even before 30th June, 1995 it would be considered as after 30th June, 1995 and TDS shall have to be made.

(iii) CBDT in Circular No. 647 dated 22nd March, 1993 [(1993) 110 CTR (St) 185] has clarified that the difference between the issue price and the face value of the commercial papers and the certificates of deposits is to be treated as "discount allowed" and not as "interest paid".

(iv) In Circular No. 65, dated 2nd September, 1971, it has been clarified that if there is no immediate discounting and the bank is acting as agent; receives on the expiry of the period the payment for the bill from the buyer on behalf of the supplier and credits it to him accordingly, it amounts to the interest paid to the bank on behalf of the supplier and buyer will have to deduct the tax from the interest.

(v) It has been held by Gujarat High Court that deduction under Section 80L will be allowable to the trust as it is an Individual [CIT vs. Deepak Family Trust No. 1 & Ors. (1994) 119 CTR (Guj) 150: (1995) 211 ITR 575 (Guj): TC 24R.225]. Following this principle Gujarat High Court in the case of M.L. Family Trust vs. State of Gujarat & Anr. (1995) 127 CTR (Guj) 407: (1995) 213 ITR 152 (Guj): TC 48R.362 has held that the status of the trustees would be same as that of beneficiaries, and if all the beneficiaries are individuals, there is no liability of trust to deduct TDS. It is also confirmed by Madras High Court in the case of ITO vs. Arihant Trust (1995) 127 CTR (Mad) 448: (1995) 214 ITR 306 (Mad): TC 5R.222.

(vi) In case of outstation sale of goods if the supplier draws a hundi on the buyer and routes it through his banker along with transport documents with instructions to deliver the documents on acceptance of hundi and to charge interest on hundi amount from the date of acceptance to the date of actual payment, the question would arise whether tax is deductible if interest charged exceeds Rs. 5,000. CBDT in Circular No. 48 dated 7th November, 1990, has clarified that the buyer has to deduct TDS in such cases.

(vii) Circular No. 65 dated 2nd September, 1971, clarifying the earlier instructions given in Circular No. 22 dated 13th May, 1968, has explained that where the supplier of goods make over the usance bill/hundi to his bank which discounts the same and credits the net amount to the supplier's account, without waiting for realisation of the bill on due date, the property in the usance bill/hundi passes on to the bank. Therefore, the eventual collection on due date is a receipt by the bank on its own behalf and not on behalf of the supplier. Therefore, such immediate discounting of usance bill is in the nature of price paid for the bill, technically is not interest and therefore no TDS is required to be deducted.

(viii) However, if there is no discounting of such usance bill by the bank, the bank merely acting as agent receives on the expiry of the period the payment of the bill from the buyer on behalf of the supplier and credits to him accordingly, what is received by the bank is interest on behalf of the supplier and in such an event the buyer will have to deduct TDS on the amount of interest.

(ix) A vessel is purchased from abroad on 180 days usance bill through a prime bank of India. When the L.C. is drawn; the interest amount is also included in the L.C. Whether it is required to deduct TDS on such amount? If yes, then who is liable to deduct TDS? The asset is purchased from a foreign party and the payment is made by the bank. The payment of interest made is strictly payment made by the bank to the foreign bank and accordingly the liability to deduct tax does not arise.

(x) Hire charges in case of Hire Purchase transactions do not attract provisions of Section 194A. In the case of Commercial Motors Finance Ltd. Vs ACIT (2002) 82 ITD 176(Inc), it has been held that in hire purchase transaction the ownership of the Vehicle remains with the hire purchase trader and the charges are paid for the use of the vehicles and for the damages caused to it and the transaction can not be said to be a money lending or financing transaction.

1.7 <u>Winnings from Lottery or Crossword Puzzle-Section 194B</u>

(a) Liability of TDS

This Section was introduced from 1st June, 1972 requiring any person responsible for paying to any person any income by way of winning from lottery or crossword puzzle exceeding Rs. 5,000 to deduct tax at source. The responsibility to deduct is on every person including individual, HUF like under Section 192 and there is no exception. As the income from winning of lottery, etc. is exempt upto 5,000 under Section 10(3), winnings above this amount is subject to TDS at 30 per cent. It is to be noted that as per provisions of Section 115BB of the Act, income by way of winnings from lottery or crossword puzzle or race including horse race or card game and other game of any sort or gambling or betting is chargeable to tax at the flat rate of 30 per cent even if the income is below the maximum amount (Rs.50, 000/- presently) not chargeable to tax.

(b) Issues

(i) Where the prize is given partly in cash and partly in kind, TDS is deductible at the aggregate amount of cash prize and the value of the prize in kind.

(ii) Earlier, if the prize given was only in kind then no income-tax was required to be deducted. But to ensure that the person receiving the prize in kind do not go away tax free, an amendment has been made from 1st June, 1997. This has been clarified by CBDT in Circular 763 dated 18th February, 1998 [(1998) 145 CTR (St) 38: (1998) 230 ITR (St) 84] that if the winnings are wholly in kind or partly in cash and partly in kind and the cash is not sufficient to meet the liability of TDS, then the person responsible for paying the winning before releasing such winnings shall ensure that tax has been paid in respect of the aggregate winnings. For this purpose, the buyer can collect the amount of TDS from the payee or ask him to pay the TDS directly and show the proof of having TDS deposited. *[See K.C. Suresh vs. Director of Lotteries & Ors. (1992) 103 CTR (Ker) 289: (1993) 199 ITR 266 (Ker): TC 5R.328].*

(iii) Various advertisements appear in the newspaper wherein prizes are given on purchase of various items. It is the duty of the seller to deduct TDS and have the record of the same. The value of winnings in kind is to be taken as the cost incurred by the buyer in acquiring the said winnings in kind as per Board Circular No.763 dt. 18.2.98 Para 51, 1, and 52.2 (1998) 230 ITR 84-85(St).

(v) If an assessee subscribes to a Chit Fund Scheme and obtains the receipts in his name taken out from a draw under which chits are taken out periodically, such scheme would also amount to lottery and liable to TDS. *[See CIT vs. Sanjiv Kumar (1980) 123 ITR 187 (P&H): TC 68R.235].*

(vi) The duty to deduct TDS under Section 194B is cast on the person responsible for paying the winnings from lottery, etc. The deduction is to be made by such person responsible at the time of the payment. In such a case it is not at the time of acceptance of the claim by the winner.

vi) Prizes on unsold lottery tickets lying with organizer of the lottery tickets on behalf of the State Government is not liable for TDS as the organizer has neither purchased the ticket nor taken any chance Commercial Corporation of India Ltd. Vs ITO (1993) 201 ITR 348(Bom), Director of State Lotteries Vs CIT and others (1999) 238 ITR(Gau).

1.8 Winnings from Horseraceing–Section 194BB

The provisions of this Section are on the line of provisions of Section 194B and therefore, not repeated; except the limit here is of Rs. 2,500. The provision of TDS is only for horse race and, therefore, prizes for motor race, etc. are not covered under this Section 194B. In horse race also, gross amount of prize money received by the owner of a horse, popularly known as 'stake money' is not be covered by definition of winnings from horse races and in such case TDS is not required to be deducted. A bookmaker in the normal parlance is a person who carries on business of receiving or negotiating bets and wagers. Whether he carries on that business on his own account or as servant or agent to any other person, it is his business and income from such business is also not covered under Section 194BB.

1.9 Payment to Contractors and Sub–contractors-Section 194C

Section 194C for deduction of tax at source on payment to contractors and sub-contractors was introduced by the Finance Act, 1972 effective from 1st April, 1972. There was no such provision in the old Income Tax Act of 1992.

After its insertion in 1972, this Section has been amended a number of times for widening the scope. The scope has been widened by including various status of the person liable to deduct as well as the nature of payments liable for deduction of tax at source. The major amendment was made by the Finance Act, 1995, effective from 1st July, 1995, The scope of the word 'contract' was expanded to include contracts for advertising, broadcasting, telecasting, carriage of goods and passengers and catering.

It is important to understand the meaning of terms "contractor, sub-contractor, work contract", etc. A number of Circulars have been issued for this and one may refer to following Circulars carefully:

Circular No. 86 dt. 29-5-1972, Circular No. 93 dt.26-9-1972, Circular No. 295 dt. 6-3- 1981, Circular No. 433 dt. 25-9-1985 [(1986) 50 CTR (St) 1], Circular No. 487 dt. 8-6- 1987 [(1987) 63 CTR (St) 37], Circular No. 502 dt. 27-1-1988 [(1988) 69 CTR (St) 3], Circular No. 505 dt. 19-2-1988 [(1988) 69 CTR (St) 4], Circular No. 558 dt. 28-3-1990 [(1989) 82 CTR (St) 404], Circular No. 713 dt. 2-8-1995 [(1995) 127 CTR (St) 9], Circular No. 714 dt. 3-8-1995 [(1995) 127 CTR (St) 9], Circular No. 715 dt. 8-8-1995 [(1995) 127 CTR (St) 13], Circular No. 716 dt. 9-8-1995 [(1995) 127 CTR (St) 18], Circular No. 720 dt. 3-8-1995 [(1995) 127 CTR (St) 82], Circular No. 723 dt. 19-9-1995 [(1995) 128 CTR (St) 6]

The word "contractor" is defined in Explanation 1 to Section 194C (2) so as to include a contractor who is carrying out any work (including supply of labour for carrying out any work) in pursuance of a contract between the contractor and foreign Government or foreign enterprise or any association or body established outside India.

For this, the Gujarat High Court judgment in the case of All Gujarat Federation of Tax Consultants vs. CBDT (1995) 126 CTR (Guj) 288 : (1995) 214 ITR 276 (Guj) : TC S5.521 is important, wherein it was held that before a person can be called as a contractor, his status must have nexus in its characteristics as carrying out work for another person as a contractor in the ordinary sense and nor merely carrying on activities of his own business or profession in the ordinary course by charging fees, remuneration, freight, etc. The Delhi High Court in the case of S.R. Finance Ltd. vs. CBDT (1994) 122 CTR (Del) 431 : (1995) 211 ITR 861 (Del) : TC S5.516 confirmed this view.

Similarly in normal understanding the term "sub-contractor" would be a person who takes a part or whole of the contract from another contractor who has taken the contract from the principal or even from another sub-contractor itself. One may refer to the important decision of ITO vs. Rama Nand & Co. (1987) 59 CTR (HP) 146: (1987) 163 ITR 702 (HP): TC 5R.341.

With regard to the expression "work" is defined in Explanation 3 to Section 194C which has now broaden the coverage of TDS so as to include :

(a) advertising;
(b) broadcasting, telecasting·
(c) carriage of goods and passengers by any mode of transport other than by railways; and
(d) catering.

Whether a contract is a work and labour contract or not is a difficult point which can be decided only by reference to actual facts of the case. But it has to be distinguished from the contract for sale of goods. Important judgments that can be referred to while deciding whether it is a 'work' or not are as under:-

29 STC 474 (SC), 16 STC 240 (SC), 42 STC 409 (SC), 38 SCT 176 (SC), 26 STC 38 (SC), 16 STC 360 (SC), 80 STC 125 (Gau) and 29 STC 474 (SC)

Associated Cement Co. Ltd. vs. CIT (1979) 11 CTR (Pat) 211 : (1979) 120 ITR 444 (Pat) : TC 5R.331

a) Liability of TDS

(i) The liability to deduct tax at source under Section 194C is on every person who is responsible for paying any sum in pursuance of a contract between the contractor and any of the 10 categories specified in Section 194C(1). As such the obligation is on every person but there has to be a contract by any of the 10 categories specified therein. That way the drafting of this Section is from that of than other sections like 192, 194A, 194BB etc. Accordingly, any one who makes payment in consequence to a contract between the contractor and the specified persons, he is required to deduct tax.

(ii) The obligation to deduct tax at source is not applicable in respect of any sum in pursuance of any contract the consideration for which does not exceed Rs.20, 000 Thus if each individual contract is not of amount exceeding Rs.20, 000, no TDS is to be deducted, though there may be number of contracts in a financial year and the aggregate value of such contract may exceed Rs.20, 000. One may refer to clarification issued by CBDT vide Circular No.715 dt. 8th August, 1995 (answer to question no.9).

(iii) The liability to deduct tax at source is not applicable if the contract is between a contractor and an individual or HUF as individual or HUF are not included in the 10 categories specified in sub-Section (1) of Section 194C.

The liability to deduct tax at source on payment to sub-contractors is on the contractor. Sub-Section (2) of Section 194C puts an obligation on the person being a contractor responsible for paying any sum in pursuance of a contract with the sub- contractor to deduct tax at source. The only exclusion is that of individual and HUF whose sales, gross receipts or turnover in business or profession is less than Rs.40 lacs or Rs.10 lacs as the case may be in the immediate preceding year. As such if contractor is an individual or HUF whose turnover is more than specified in the immediate preceding year, it will be required to deduct tax at source on payment to sub-contractors if the consideration of the contract exceeds Rs. 20,000.

(b) Amount of TDS

(i) The deduction is required to be made at the rate of 2 per cent at the time of credit or payment whichever is earlier. But in the case of advertising contract it is only 1 per cent. The important thing to note here is that deduction in regard to this point shall apply when an advertiser makes payment to an advertising agent. But if advertising agency make payments to their models, artists, photographers etc. the provisions of Section 194J would apply and the rate would be 5 per cent.

(ii) Rate of TDS is 1 per cent in case of credit or payment to sub-contractor. The tax shall have to be deducted at source either at the time of credit to the account of the payee (by whatever name called including suspense account) or at the time of payment whichever is earlier.

(iii) Deduction on supply contracts

Contracts for the construction of buildings or dams or laying of roads are in the nature of contracts for work and labour and tax is to be deducted from payments made in respect of such contracts. Similarly, contracts given for processing of goods also are in the nature of works contract. Where however the contractor undertakes to supply any item fabricated according to the specification given by the specified person and the property in such item passes to such person only after such item is delivered, the contract will be a contract for sale and outside the purview of Section 194C. In the case of State of Punjab Vs Associated Hotels of India Ltd.(1972)29STC474(SC), it has been held that where the principal objective of work undertaken by the payee of the price is not the transfer of a chattel qua chattel the contract is of work and labour. The test is whether or not the work and labour bestowed; end in anything that can properly become the subject of sale. Where the intention plainly is not to sell the article but to improve the land in a building contract or the other chattel, and the consideration is not for the transfer of chattel but for labour and work done and the materials furnished, the contract will be one of work and labour.

(iv) Whether deduction on gross amount or net amount

The TDS is to be made on the gross payment to contractors or the net payment after deduction on account of materials supplied by the contractor, is to be decided on the basis of the terms of the contract. Where the contractor has undertaken to construct a building or dam and the govt. or other person has agreed to supply material necessary for carrying out the work, the deduction will be on gross payment. However, where the contractor agrees to provide labour for the work, and the ownership of materials supplied remains at all times with the other person, the deduction will be only on the amount paid to contractor for providing labour for the work. The above clarification was issued by the Board vide circular no.86 dt. 29.5.1972. As per circular no.295 dt.6.3.1981, it has been again clarified that TDS is to be deducted on gross payment i.e. including cost of material supplied by the government or any other specified person. The circular clarifies the judgement of the Supreme Court in the case of Brij Bhushan Lal Parduman Kumar Vs CIT (1978) 115 ITR 524(SC) and Patna High Court in Associated Cement Company Ltd. Vs CIT (1979) 120 ITR 444(Pat) whereby it was held that for computing the income of the contractor, the cost of the material supplied by the Government can not be included as there could not be a theoretical possibility of any profit being made on such supplies. It has been reiterated in this circular that circular no.86 dt. 29.5.1972 shall continue to apply to determine the liability for tax deduction at source.

(v) Composite Contract for work done

In a recent judgement in the case of Essar Oil Ltd. Vs ITO (2001) 77 ITD 92(Rajkot), it has been held by the ITAT that construction of oil refinery plant is a composite contract and despite splitting of the contract into three parts of i.e. supply of equipment and material, labour cum erection, and construction of refinery, the contract was a composite contract and tax is to be deducted on the total amount.

(c) Issues

(i) How does one decide the limit of Rs. 20,000?

If the first contract in the month of April is of Rs. 15,000 no TDS provisions shall apply. But again if the payer and the contractor, say in the month of May have another contract of Rs. 10,000, can the limit of Rs. 20,000 apply to this second contract? The limit of Rs. 20,000 applies to each contract whether oral or written and therefore, each contract being separate and each being less than Rs. 20,000, the liability of TDS does not apply even on such subsequent events of payment or payments to the same party.

(ii) As provided in Section 196, the provision of TDS shall not apply for any payment to Government, Government Corporations, Reserve Bank of India, which are exempt from income–tax as well as to mutual funds.

(iii) Though the Chapter of TDS envisages the deduction of tax 'from the income' in the hands of the recipient, in case of contractor, TDS is to be made on the amount of contract and not on the income involved in such contract.

(iv) It has been clarified by the Board in Circular Nos. 714 and 715 that provisions of TDS will not apply when advertising agency makes the payment to the media which includes both print and electronic media. But as TDS at 5 per cent is to be deducted while making payment to artists, etc. the situation is confusing inasmuch as in actual practice the advertising agencies recover the cost of advertisements from their clients. This is subject to TDS at 1 per cent. An advertising agent always makes payment to media after deducting their commission. Therefore, it is difficult to understand as to how media will deduct 5 per cent from the above commission. If such deduction is made, the advertising agents will suffer double deduction on their commission income i.e. once at the rate of 1 per cent under Section 194C and again under Section 194J at 5 per cent.

(v) In the case of travel agents, provisions of Section 194C do not apply to payments made to airlines, steamer, bus, etc. or to the travel agents for purchase of tickets for individuals. But if payments are made for chartering an aircraft, steamer, bus, etc. for carriage of passengers or goods then tax shall have to be deducted under Section 194C.

(vi) For clearing and forwarding agents also it is clarified that such agents act as independent contractors and, therefore, when any payment for freight, custom duty or other charges is made to them, tax will have to be deducted under Section 194C. Further, when such clearing and forwarding agents make payments of freight to the airline, ship, transport company, etc., they will have to deduct tax at source under Section 194C. Thus unnecessary hardship is created. This is because when the company appoints clearing and forwarding agent, such an agent is the agent of company. As such, when he makes payment for freight, duty, etc. it is always on behalf of the company and there should not be any liability of TDS on him. Accordingly, such company should be made liable to TDS from the amount of service charges payable to clearing and forwarding agent and there should be no obligation for TDS on the amount representing freight, duty, etc. which is collected by clearing and forwarding agent in the form of reimbursement of expenses.

(vii) In the case of tour operator, it cannot be said that he is the agent of any airline, shipping company or transport company. He merely organises the tour for group of persons and gives services of booking of tickets, hotels, local transport, etc. Since the major portion of tour operator's charges will be covered by the above inclusive definition of "work" as defined in Section 194C, persons making payment to tour operator in excess of Rs. 20,000 are also required to make TDS.

(viii) Another area covered now is that of catering. Catering normally includes provision of food, beverages, etc. on function like conference, seminars, marriages, social functions, public meetings etc. If such functions are held in a hotel, the charges are not for the hall or rooms, but mainly for providing such food or beverages. Therefore, on the entire payment to hotel for such functions, tax has to be deducted. In a recent case it has been held that hotel cannot distinguish the charges of food and other charges for ambience, music etc. while collecting charges from the customers as printed in the menu card. However in normal course, when a payment in a restaurant of a hotel bill paid is more than Rs. 20,000, no liability of TDS would arise.

(ix) Couriers are also now covered under the provisions of Section 194C and for work done of carriage of document or lease is to be considered in the nature of carriage of goods and TDS is required to be deducted.

(x) Payments to recruitment agents are in the nature of payment of services rendered and not of contract. The firm of chartered accountants or legal consultants doing such work and others will be covered under definition of Section 194J and rate of TDS will be 5 per cent in such cases. Similar shall be the situation of payments made by the company to share registrar as well as the brokerage and commission paid to the agents procuring fixed deposits, etc. if the services provided are in nature of professional or technical services under the agency agreement.

It is significant to note that as per Section 194H TDS is to be deducted on payment of commission or brokerage. Therefore, brokerage and commission paid to any agency cannot be subject to TDS under Section 194C.

(xi) To cover the sponsorship by advertisement for debates, conference, seminars, etc., it is clarified that provisions of Section 194C shall apply for payments made for sponsorship of such conference, seminars, debates and other functions held/ organised in schools, colleges or associations as it is with a view to earn publicity through display of banners, etc.

(xii) Electricians and plumbers are also covered under Section 194C, if payments made to them is for a contract the value of which exceeds Rs. 20,000. In the same manner payments for routine or normal maintenance contracts which may also include supply of spare parts are also covered by Section 194C. If such work involves technical services then they will be covered under Section 194J.

1.10 Insurance Commission–Section 194D

This is one of the Sections which have not been amended since inception from 1st April, 1973 except by way of insertion of second proviso with effect from 1st June, 1987. The Section provides that any person responsible for paying to a resident in India any income by way of insurance commission is required to deduct income-tax at source at the rate of 10 per cent (20 per cent in the case of company). The liability would arise provided commission credited or paid in a financial year exceeds Rs.5000 during the financial year.

1.11 Sections 194E, 194EE, 194F, 194K, 196A, 196B, 196C & 196D.

(i) The provisions of TDS are applicable for payments made to non-resident sportsman who is not a citizen of India, non resident sports association and institution as envisaged under Section 194E at the rate of 10 per cent.

(ii) There is a liability of deduction of tax at source on payment made in respect of deposits under National Savings Scheme (NSS) under Section 194EE. No liability arises if payments to the payee during the financial year is less than Rs. 2,500. Moreover, the provisions of this Section does not apply to the payment of the said amount to the heirs of the assessee.

(iii) Section 194F cast responsibility to TDS on payments made on account of re-purchase of units of Mutual Fund or Unit Trust of India at the rate of 20 per cent.

(iv) Section 194K is in respect of deduction of tax at source on payment of income to a resident in respect of units of Mutual Fund specified under Section 10(23D) or of the Unit Trust of India at the rate of 10 per cent in case the amount of such income credited or paid exceeds Rs.2500. However, this provision is not applicable on income credited or paid on or after 1st April, 2003 since distribution tax of 12.5 per cent has been levied under Section 115-R of the Act on income distribution by Mutual Fund and Unit Trust of India. The tax on distribution is to be deposited within 14 days from the date of distribution or payment whichever is earlier. The UTI and the Mutual Fund is required to submit an annual return in form 63 and 63A respectively by 15th September each year giving details of the income distributed and the tax paid thereon. The return is to be certified by a Chartered Accountant.

(v) Sections 196A and 196B provide for deduction of tax at source from the income in respect of units to non-resident and offshore fund, Section 196C provides for deduction of tax at source from income from foreign currency bonds or shares of Indian company and Section 196D is with reference to TDS from income of Foreign Institutional Investors from securities.

1.12 Commission on Sale of Lottery Tickets –Section 194G

i) The provisions of TDS are applicable with effect from 1st October, 1991 on a person responsible for paying to any person, stocking, distributing, purchasing or selling lottery tickets, any income by way of commission, remuneration or prize(by whatever name called) on such tickets, if the amount exceeds Rs.1000. The deduction is to be made at the rate of 10 per cent at the time of credit or payment whichever is earlier.

ii) Liability to deduct tax under this Section is applicable for every person and there is no exclusion of individual or HUF. For deduction the payment made should be in the nature of commission, remuneration or prize arising from sale of lottery tickets.

iii) The 'commission' prima facie is a payment made to an agent for an agency work or a remuneration paid to an agent for an agency work other than salary. Remuneration here in this Section means something paid to a person doing a business in purchase, sale, distribution or stocking of lottery tickets. 'Prize' is a reward or incentive for lottery tickets winning any announced lottery amount.

iv) Commission is distinct from discount. The discount allowed on sale of lottery tickets is not covered by the provisions of Section 194G. In the case of M.S.Hameed and others Vs Director of State Lotteries & Ors (2001) 249 ITR 186(Ker), it was held that sale of Lottery ticket at a discount on a slab system is not the transaction to be the one in the contemplation of Section #194G of the Act.

Unlike Sections 194B and 194BB, in this Section a payee can make an application to the Assessing Officer for Nil or lower rate of TDS under Section 197 of the Act.

1.13 Commission or Brokerage – Section 194H

a) Liability of TDS

i) The provision of tax deduction at source on payment of commission or brokerage were initially introduced by the Finance (No.2) Act, 1999 with effect from 1.10.1991, but were withdrawn with effect from 31.5.92. The present provision were reinserted by the Finance Act, 2001 effective from 1st June, 2001.

ii) The liability to deduct tax at source is on every person other than an individual or HUF whose sales, gross receipts or turnover in business or profession does not exceed the monetary limit specified under Section 44AB of the Act in the immediate preceding financial year. The rate of deduction is five per cent (with effect from 1.6.2002). Earlier the rate was 10 per cent (from 1.6.2001 to 31.5.2002). However no deduction is to be made if the aggregate amount credited or paid during the financial year does not exceed Rs.2500.

iii) Commission or brokerage include any payment for services rendered in the course of buying or selling of goods or in relation to any transaction relating to any asset, valuable article or thing. However, commission does not include professional services as defined and notified under Section 44AA of the Act. Commission or brokerage for buying or selling securities and insurance commission are specifically excluded from the purview of Section 194-H. Securities includes shares, bonds, debentures, derivatives, units, government securities, other notified securities and rights or interests in securities.

(b) Issues

i) In the case of ACIT Vs Samaj (2001) 77 ITD 358(Cuttack) it has been held that sale of news papers to agents at discounted price is not covered by this provision as agents were collecting proceeds from hawkers and were also responsible for unsold copies. As such there was no element of agency in the arrangement. The mere use of word commission does not convert a relationship of vendor and vendee into one of agency.

ii) Similar is the case of commission to advertising agents. The true relationship of the parties is to be gathered from the nature of the contract, its terms and conditions as has been held by the Supreme Court in the case of Sri Tirumala Venkateshwara Timber and Bambo Firm Vs CTO AIR 1968 SC 784.

iii) Sale of discount made available to stamp vendors does not fall within the definition of 'commission' or brokerage Ahmedabad Stamp Vendors Association Vs Union of India (2002) 257 ITR 202(Guj).

1.14 <u>Rent–Section 194-I</u>

(a) Liability of TDS

i) The liability to deduct tax at source from the payment of rent was introduced under Section 194-I with effect from 1st June, 1994. The Section is applicable only if the rent payable exceeds Rs. 1, 20,000 during the financial year. Liability to deduct tax is on every person other than an individual or HUF whose sales, gross receipts or turnover in business or profession does not exceed the monetary limits prescribed under Section 44AB of the Act in the immediate preceding financial year.

ii) TDS is to be deducted when the rent is paid or credited whichever is earlier at the rate of 15 per cent if payment is made to an individual or HUF and at the rate of 20 per cent, if made to other person.

iii) The definition of rent is very wide and covers any lease, sub-lease, tenancy or any other agreement or arrangement for use of any land or any building (including factory building) together with furniture, fittings and land appurtenant thereto, whether or not such building is owned by the payee. Thus not only the owner but even the sub-tenant is covered. Similarly not only residential and office and the commercial premises but even godown and warehouses are also covered. Moreover payments made for hotel accommodation, hoarding on the buildings, payment made to business centre, payment made to ceremony halls, halls or rooms of the clubs or associations etc. are also covered. It is not important what nomenclature is given to the payments made. If the payment is towards use of any land or building the liability shall arise.

iv) The liability of TDS is there only if the credit or the payment to the payee is more than Rs. 1,20,000 during the financial year. Therefore, if payer is one and if land or building is owned by co-owners and if each one is paid Rs. 1,20,000 per annum, no liability of TDS shall arise. The controversial issue had arisen in the case of Smt. Bishakha Sarkar (1996) 219 ITR 327 (Cal) wherein the Calcutta High Court, with utmost respect, adopted a different view that provisions of Section 194-I applies qua premises and not qua recipient of the rent. However the Board in its circular No.715 dt.8th August, 1995 has clarified that if there are a number of payees each having a definite and ascertainable share in the property, the limit of Rs.1, and 20,000 will apply to each of the payee separately.

(b) Issues

i) Rent paid to government or to local authorities and statutory bodies whose income is exempt under Sections 10(20) and 10(20A) is outside the purview of TDS as per Board Circular No.699 dt.30.1.1995 (1995)212 ITR 2(St).

ii) Payment made by a film distributor to cinema hall owner (film exhibitor) is also not liable for composite services as cinema hall is not let out to the distributor and payment is for composite services and there is no lease or tenancy. Board Circular No.736 dt. 13.2.1976(1996) 218 ITR 97(St).

iii) If there is a composite agreement for paying specified percentage based on turnover but in essence the agreement is for taking the premises on rent, the tax is liable to be deducted on such payment. However, in the case of Kamat Hotel (I) Ltd. Vs ITO (2001) 78 ITD 241 (Mum) , it was held that royalty/ commission paid to the owners as a percentage of daily receipts was fluctuating and the dominant intention was conduct of business not mere letting out. Applying the ratio of the decision given in an old case of Indian Radio & Cable Communication Co. Ltd. vs CIT(1937) 5 ITR 270 (PC) and Gopinath Vir Bhan vs CIT 6 ITR 243(Lah) it was held that rent can not be of a variable amount.

iv) Tax is deductible where hotel room are hired on regular basis for a period which may be less than a year but the amount payable exceeds Rs.1, 20,000. in a financial year The hotel accommodation taken on regular basis has been clarified to mean earmarked rooms let out for a specified rate and a specified period or where a room or set of rooms are not earmarked but the hotel has a legal obligation to provide such types of room during the currency of the agreement. However, where an agreement is merely in the nature of rate contract, it will not be accommodation taken on regular basis and TDS provision will not be applicable. CBDT Circular No.5 dt. 30th July, 2002.

v) Rent from leasing out of a factory building though assessable on business income, will be liable for tax deduction at source. TDS under Section 194-I applies even if rent receipt is assessable as business income. F.No.275/108/95-IT (B) dt. 27.2.1997. But lease of storage tanks for storing oil is not covered; Gulf Oil India Ltd. Vs ITO (2000) 75 ITD 172(Mum). Tax is to be deducted on non-refundable deposit since such deposit is rent. However, refundable security deposit is not covered.

vi) If the furniture is inbuilt in the premises, but the owner or sub-owner is separate, and if the payer makes separate payment for the use of such furniture and fixtures and separate payment to another person for rent of building, then the limit of Rs. 1,20,000 and liability would arise qua payment to the payee of building rent only.

vii) Irrespective of the interest-free deposits given to the owner, the liability of TDS arises only when payment of rent exceeds Rs.1, 20,000. The amount of interest-free deposit can not be converted into the rent equivalent to increase the amount of rent.

viii) Though godown, factory building and warehousing charges are included under the provisions of this Section, payment made to cold storage for preserving vegetables, milk, ice-cream, potato or onions, etc. are payments made for hiring of plant and machinery and not for building CIT vs Yamuna Cold Storage (1981) 129 ITR 728 (P & H) However, in view of the Supreme Court judgment in the case of Delhi Cold Storage (P) Ltd. vs. CIT (1991) 191 ITR 656 (SC), whereby it has been held that running a cold storage plant does not amount to manufacturing or processing of goods, it is felt that payment to cold storage would be covered under the provisions of Section 194-I. The Board in its circular No.718 dt.22.8.1995 has clarified that warehousing charges are subject to TDS.

ix) If there is a composite agreement whereby various kinds of services like caretaking, water, air-conditioner and other things are provided and if service charges are not specifically seggregated or defined, then tax will be deductible under Section 194-I on the whole payment. But if such service charges can be seggregated and are made by separate agreement or working, then on such payments no tax is required to be deducted.

x) It is important to note that amount of Rs. 1, 20,000 shall be towards rent which may include municipal taxes, etc. Therefore, if municipal taxes are to be borne by the tenant then limit of Rs. 1, 20,000 will be to the exclusion of the municipal taxes borne by the tenant and no TDS is to be deducted on such municipal taxes.

1.15 Professional and Technical Services–Section 194J

(a) Liability of TDS

i) Tax deduction at source was extended on fees for professional and technical services by inserting Section 194J in the Act with effect from 1st July, 1995. Earlier the CBDT had tried to cover these payments by extending the scope of Section 194C through the Circular No.681 dt. 8.3.1994. The definition of 'work' in Section 194C was defined to include all types of contracts including transport contracts, service contracts which was to include services rendered by lawyers, doctors, engineers etc. But various high courts held that circular to be ultra vires. Thereafter the Act was amended and the present Section 194J was introduced to cover payment of fees for professional or technical services for TDS.

ii) The obligation to deduct tax at source is on all persons except individual and HUF whose turnover, gross receipts or sales in the business is less than the monetary limits prescribed under Section 44AB of the Act in the immediate preceding financial year. The tax rate prescribed is 5 per cent. The liability arises if the payment exceeds Rs.20, 000 in a financial year.

iii) Professional service has been defined to mean "services rendered by a person in the course of carrying on legal, medical, engineering, architectural, profession or the profession of accountancy or technical consultancy or interior decoration or advertising or such other profession as is notified by the Board for the purpose of Section 44AA or of this Section".

(iv) So far the following professions have been notified by CBDT under Section 44AA by notification dated 12th January, 1977 and dated 25.9.1992.

- Accountancy, Archictectural, Engineering, Legal, Medical, Interior decoration.

-Authorised representatives.

-Film artists like actor, cameraman, director, music director, etc.

-Chartered secretary.

- Technical Consultancy.

"Fees for technical services" shall have the same meaning as in Explanation 2 to Section 9(1)(vii) of the Act; i.e., "any consideration (including any lumpsum consideration) for the rendering of any managerial, technical or consultancy services (including the provisions of services of technical or other personnel) but does not include consideration for any construction, assembly, mining or like project undertaken by the recipient or consideration which would be the income of the recipient or consideration which would be the income of the recipient chargeable under the head "Salaries".

Thus the scope of Section is very wide and covers fees paid to merchant bankers, consultants for financial services, consultants for raising finance for obtaining loans from banks and financial institutions, etc.

(b) Issues

i) The Finance Act, 2003 has exempted with effect from 1.6.2003 individual and HUF from deducting tax at source on payment of professional fee for personal purposes of such individual or any member of HUF. This exemption is only to individual and HUF and that too from payment of professional fee. The objective is to exempt payment of doctor's fee and lawyer's fee in connection with personal matters.

ii) The Board vide Circular No.715 dt. 8th August, 1995 has clarified that TDS is applicable on the gross amount as the word is used any sum paid and reimbursement of expenses can not be reduced from the bill amount for the TDS. In the case of ACC Ltd. Vs CIT 1979 120 ITR 444(Pat) it has been held that tax is deductible from the sum paid not from net income. The Board Circular No.295 dt.6.3.1981 and circular no.86 DT. 29.5.1972 issued for Section 194C has clarified that tax is to be deduced on the gross payment including cost of material supplied by the government or any other specified person.

iii) Royalty paid to authors is outside the purview of Section 194J. The scope of TDS can be widened by subjecting payment of royalty liable for TDS.

iv) In the case of professionals like chartered accountants and tax consultants, the usual method of accounting is cash system. As per the provisions of Section 194J tax is to be deducted at source from the amount credited by the payer to the account of professional or to fees payable account. On receipt of the bill, the payer following accrual method of accounting credits the amount but makes payment in the subsequent year. As per Section 199, credit for TDS shall be given in the assessment year in which such income is assessable. Since payment of fee in such case will be offered for taxation in the next year, the credit of TDS will be allowed in next year only. No problem should arise with regard to the date of certificate issued and the year in which such credit is claimed for such TDS as language of Section 199 is clear. Moreover the CBDT has issued circular No.5 of 2001 on rent whereby the above view has been clarified with reference to credit of TDS deducted on payment of rent in somewhat similar circumstances.

v) The provision is more stringent because difficulties are faced by professional partnership firms where tax is deducted under Section 194J from the firm. The professional firms pay salary and interest to the partners which are allowed as deduction and so assessed as partner's individual income. But as TDS would be deducted from the firm the firm will have to claim refund of TDS, whereas partners will have to pay advance tax. There is substantial difference in the rate of interest between the interest receivable on refund and interest payable on short-fall of advance tax. The only option is to obtain the certificate from the Assessing Officer for lower rate of tax and pay advance tax on income of partners.

1.16 Payment to Non Residents– Section 195

Payments made to non residents are liable for TDS under Section 195. Any person responsible for paying to a non-resident, not being a company or a foreign company any interest or any other sum chargeable under the provisions of this Act, is liable to deduct TDS at the rates which are in force. These provisions are wide enough to cover and include all amounts chargeable to tax except which relates to salaries. As per second proviso re-inserted with effect from 1st April, 2003, dividends which are subject-matter of Section 115-O are excluded and, therefore, no tax is deductible from dividend which are declared and distributed by Indian companies.

(a) Liability of TDS

The obligation to deduct tax at source is on any person. But that does not mean it includes a foreign company or non resident. Primarily, legislation of a country has territorial jurisdiction. Circular No. 726 dt. 18.10.95 specifically exempts non residents/foreign companies not having agent/business connection/ Permanent Establishment in India from withholding tax (TDS) under Section 194J from payments made to professionals. In the case of Shri Kumar Poddar Vs DCIT 59 TTJ 304(Mum) it has been held that Section 195 does not apply to payments by one non-resident to another non resident outside India. There are judgements of Authority for Advance Ruling whereby it has been held that obligation of the 'person' in the Act includes non resident and foreign company and therefore the provisions of Section 195 are applicable to non-residents 235ITR565(AAR) and 228ITR487(AAR).

(b) Issues

i) Liability to deduct tax is only on that sum to non-resident which is chargeable to tax under the provisions of the Act. If the sum being paid is not chargeable to tax, because of provisions of the Act or Double Taxation Avoidence Agreement, there is no liability to deduct tax at source DCIT Vs Tata Yodogawa Ltd.(1999) 68 ITD 47 (Pat). It is to be noted that Section 9 of the Act is a deeming provision whereby certain income is deemed to accrue or arise in India and is chargeable to tax under the Act.

ii) Tax is to be deducted at the rates in force. These rates are the rates specified in the Finance Act of the relevant year or the rates specified in an agreement entered into under Section 90. As per Board Circular No.728 dt. 30.10.1995, tax should be deducted at the rates provided in the DTAA, or the Finance Act, whichever is more beneficial to the assessee. A chart of the rates prescribed under DTAA with different countries with relevant Article No. of the DTAA is given in the Appendix-III

iii) The liability to deduct tax arises only when income is credited to the account of the payee or an actual payment which is earlier. Mere accrual of income, in the hands of a foreign company is not sufficient to fasten liability of TDS under Section 195 of the Act. CJ International Ltd. VS ITD (TDS) 79 ITD 506(Del). However, in the case of United Breweries Ltd. Vs ACIT (1995) 211 ITR 256(Kar), it has been held that liability under Section 195 arises as soon as an entry is made in the books of accounts. It has been held that even if there are debit entries in the books or if the payee ceases to be a non resident subsequently while payment is being made, the liability to Section 195 would still be there.

iv) In case of failure to deduct or pay the tax deducted on payment to non-resident, the expenditure is not allowable while computing business income as per provisions of Section 40(a) of the Act.

v) No tax is required to be deducted at source on payment of commission to non resident agents for procuring export orders as services are rendered outside India Circular No.786 dt. 7.2.2000.

vi) No tax is required to be deducted at source if the sum paid is liable to tax as per the provisions of the Act but exempt as per provisions of DTAA.

vii) To dispense with the requirement of no objection certificate from Income Tax Authorities for remittance to non residents as required by Reserve Bank of India an undertaking in duplicate to pay the shortfall in tax, if any, along with certificate from a chartered accountant is required. The performa of the undertaking and the CA certificate has been revised vide Circular No.10/2002 dt. 9.10.2002.

1.17 Rates of Tax Deduction

Rates of tax deduction at source for various payments are tabulated in Appendix-I.

1.18 Payment of Tax Deducted at Source

The tax deducted is to be paid by the deductor within one week from the last date of the month in which the deduction is made. However, where sum is credited on the last date upto which accounts are made, then payment can be made within two months of the expiration of the month in which that date falls. This extended period is not applicable for tax deducted from salaries, dividend, winning from lottery, horserace, repayment of NSS, purchase of units of mutual fund.

This is to be noted that time period for deposit of tax deducted from salaries has been extended to within one week from the last date of the month in which deduction is made by notification dt. 31st July, 2003 as against earlier time period of one week from the date of deduction.

1.19 Issue of TDS Certificates

(i) Certificate for tax deducted from salaries is to be issued in Form No.16. All other TDS certificates are to be issued in Form No.16A. The certificate is to be issued within a period of one month from the end of the month during which credit or the sum has been paid. However, in case where sum is credited on the last date upto which accounts are made, then certificate can be issued within a week after the expiry of two months in which income is so credited.

(ii) Where more than one certificate is required to be issued then at the request of the payee consolidated certificate can be issued within one month from the close of financial year.

(iii) As regards issue of TDS certificate, the date of which is linked to due date of deduction not with deposit of tax, there is practical difficulty in case tax deducted is not deposited before the last date of issue of certificate. In such a situation the practical view is to issue TDS certificate without mentioning the date of deposit of tax with the remark that tax is still to be deposited and later on to make an endorsement on the certificate or issue a separate certificate, confirming payment of tax indicated in the TDS certificate. Otherwise non deposit of tax can also be a reasonable ground in the penalty proceedings for late issue of TDS certificate.

(iv) In case TDS certificate is lost, the deductor can issue a duplicate certificate, but the credit shall be allowed only after verification by the concerned assessing officer and after obtaining indemnity bond from the assessee.

1.20 Filing of TDS Returns

The tax deductor as mentioned earlier is also required to file returns of the tax deducted. Earlier there were different forms for filing returns in respect of tax deduction from various types of payments. By notification dt. 31st July, 2003, various return forms have been consolidated. Form No.24 is the prescribed TDS return for Salaries, Form No.26 is the consolidated TDS return for all types of payments to residents other than salaries and Form No.27 is the TDS return for tax deducted from non residents. The TDS returns are to be filed annually except TDS return of tax deducted from non-residents which is to be filed quarterly within 14 days from the end of the relevant quarter. The due date of annual return both for salaries and other payments has now been fixed as 30th June. The due date for filing TDS return of salaries which was earlier 31st May, has also been fixed to 30th June. All companies with effect from 1st

June, 2003 are required to file TDS return on computers media only along with a statement in Form No.27A.

For the sake of convenience various due date for deposit of tax, issue of certificates and filing of returns have been tabulated in the Appendix-II.

1.21 Credit of Tax Deducted

The tax deducted is considered as payment of tax on behalf of the payee. As per provision of Section 199, the credit of such tax shall be given on the production of the certificate furnished under Section 203 and in the assessment year in which such income is assessable. The production of TDS certificate for obtaining credit is essential. However, under Section 205, there is bar against direct demand on the assessee to the extent to which tax has been deducted. Accordingly, in a situation where tax has been deducted, but either not deposited or certificate not issued by the deductor, then the recipient of such income can not claim credit or refund of such tax. But demand, if any, to the extent of tax deducted even in the absence of deposit of tax by the deductor or TDS certificate can not be pressed in view of the provisions of Section 205. The above view has been upheld by the Gauhati High Court in the case of Asstt. CIT & Ors Vs Om Parkash Gattani (2000) 242 ITR 638(Gau)

1.22 Recovery of Tax and Levy of Interest

As per provisions of Section 201(1) of the Act, if the person required to deduct tax at source fails to deduct the whole or any part of tax or after deducting fails to pay the tax then such person is deemed to be an assessee in default in respect of such person. Besides, the tax under Section 201(1A), such person is also liable to pay interest at the rate of 12 per cent per annum (reduced from 15 per cent with effect from 8th September, 2003) on the amount of such tax from the date on which such tax was deductible to the date on which such tax is actually paid.

In case tax has been paid directly by the deductee, than the same can not be again recovered from the deductor. There are number of judgements holding that the short fall made good on regular assessment by the concerned person wipes out the jurisdiction over the person responsible for tax deduction at source under Section 201 of the Act CIT Vs M.P.Agro Morarji Fertilizers Ltd. 176 ITR 282(MP), Grindlays Bank Ltd. Vs CIT 193 ITR 457 (Cal).

However, for levy of interest in such a situation there are conflicting judgements. The Rajasthan High Court in the case of CIT Vs Rathi Gum Industries(1995) 213 ITR 98(Raj) held that interest is to compensate the Revenue for the loss which it suffered on account of late receipt of tax. The court held that if the tax has already been paid by the recipient on such income, it may not be justified to recover the said amount of tax, but so far the liability of interest is concerned that can not be considered to be non-existent.

The Gujarat High Court in the case of CIT Vs Rishikesh Apartments Co-operative Housing Society Ltd. (2002) 253 ITR 310(Guj) however, has held that in case tax has been paid by the recipient, then such tax has to be deducted from the gross tax that the assessee should have deducted while computing interest chargeable under Section 201(1A) of the Act.

1.23 Certificate for Deduction at Lower Rate

To mitigate the hardship which one may face on deduction of tax at source at a rate which may be higher than the tax rate justified is one's case, Section 197 authorises assessing officer to issue certificate for deduction of tax at rate lower than prescribed or even no deduction of tax. The certificate can not be issued for payment of income by way of lottery (194B), horse race (194BB), non resident sportsman (194E), payment of deposits under NSS (194EE) and repurchase of units of mutual (194K). The application is to be made in prescribed Form No.13. With the amendments made by the Finance Act, 2003, provisions for issue of certificate of lower rate of deduction under Section 194C, 194G and 194J have been merged in Section 197(1).

Prescribed application form no.13, 13C, 13D, 13E and 27F have been omitted and a new consolidated form 13 has been notified with effect from 1st October, 2003. Similarly, prescribed certificate to be issued by the assessing officer in Form no.15, 15AA, 15B, 15E and 27G have been omitted with effect from 1st October, 2003. No new form has been notified. The A.O can now issue certificate by way of a letter.

1.24 Declaration Form for No Deduction of Tax

Certain income can be received without deduction of tax at source in case tax computed on the estimated total income comes to NIL. The benefit of this exemption is available under Section 197A. As per sub-Section (1) of Section 197A, exemption is available to a resident individual in respect of payment in the nature of dividend (Section 194) and payment of NSS (Section 194EE) on furnishing a declaration in the prescribed form.

As per sub-Section (1A) of Section 197A, the benefit of receiving payment without deduction of tax at source is available to a person other than a company or a firm in respect of payment in the nature of interest on securities(Section 193), interest other than interest on securities(Section 194A), and income in respect of units(Section 194K).

The prescribed form is 15G both for sub-Section 197A (1) and 197A (1A). The earlier form no.15H has been merged with this new form 15-G. The form is to be submitted in duplicate to the person responsible for the payment who in turn is required to submit one copy of the declaration to the Commissioner on or before the seventh day of the month next following the month in which the declaration is furnished.

However, this declaration can not be submitted where the amount of the income or the aggregate of the amounts of such income credited or paid during the year exceeds the maximum amount not chargeable to tax. The senior citizens, have been given the benefit of submitting declaration in new form no.15-H even if the amount or the aggregate of the amount of the nature referred above exceeds the maximum amount not chargeable to tax, in case tax computed on estimated total income of the year will be Nil. The benefit of no deduction on submission of declaration is not available in respect of income in the nature of rent, commission, fee for professional or technical services etc. To avoid hardship, it is suggested that scope of declaration be extended to cover these types of payments.

1.25 Interest and Penalty

The deductor not only has to deduct the tax, pay the same to the Government, but is also to issue the certificate and file the returns and if there is delay or default either in deduction or in payment or in following the procedures penalty and prosecution are provided.

Issues

(i) Levy of interest as such is compensatory in nature. Therefore, it is mandatory in this Act.

(ii) For calculating interest payable by the assessee in default, the procedure is laid down in rule 119A, which requires the interest to be rounded off to a whole month or fraction of a month and also to the nearest multiple of Rs. 100.

(iii) It is to be noted that there is no prescribed time–limit for passing an order levying interest. Strictly it should be within one month. But there are cases whereby order levying interest is passed even after more than ten years.

(iv) Order charging interest under Section 201 is appealable under Section 246A (1) (ha) of the Income-tax Act. Though there are decisions by some courts that because an appeal is provided it does not mean that appellate authority can go into the reasonableness of the causes in all cases.

(v) As charging of interest is mandatory there is no provision either in the Act or in the Rule or any Circular of CBDT giving any right to any authority to waive the interest levied or leviable under this provision, even if there are sufficient and good reasons.

(vi) There is no liability of TDS if the receipt is exempt in the hands of the recipient and in such cases interest under Section 201 cannot be charged.

(vii) Even if full tax is recovered by the department, for delay of payment, interest under Section 201 is leviable.

(viii) There are no powers like under rule 40 or rule 117A for waiver of interest and the only course left is appeal.

(ix) If there are variances of TDS in respect of each month in case of salaries on account of adjustment made under Section 192, no interest under Section 201 can be levied.

(x) The penalty for failure to deduct or pay the whole or any part of tax is imposable under Section 271C of the Act. The amount of penalty can be a sum equal to the amount of tax which one failed to deduct or pay. The penalty can be imposed only by the joint commissioner. The penalty order should always be a speaking order as it is different from assessment proceedings. The assessee can adduce evidences and reasonable cause during such penalty proceedings.

(xi) As in the case of interest, there is no time limit provided for levy of penalty. However, a show-cause notice initiating penalty proceedings is a must and the same should be issued within reasonable time. Once having initiated such proceedings, the same has to be completed within 6 months from the end of the month in which action for imposition of penalty is initiated as provided under Section 275.

1.26 Prosecution

(i) Chapter XXII of the Act contains provisions relating to prosecution. These are to be tried according to the provisions of Criminal Procedure Code. Such offences can be tried by a Court of law, not inferior to that of a first class presidency Magistrate. Such prosecution proceedings under Section 279 can be always at the instance of Commissioner of Income–Tax. The assessee on default is punishable with imprisonment from 3 months to 7 years.

(ii) Section 276B earlier had the words "without reasonable cause or excuse", which have been removed now and by insertion of Section 278AA, the assessee cannot be punished for aforesaid failures if he proves that there was a reasonable cause for such failure. The onus of providing the existence of reasonable cause is now on the taxpayer.

(iii) Normally prosecution should be done only in the case where tax is deducted but not paid. Merely for delay of TDS payment no prosecution should be filed. This was the view of Calcutta High Court in the case of Vinar & Co. (1992) 193 ITR 300 (Cal). But contrary view has been held by Madras High Court in the case of Rayala Corporation (P) Ltd. & Anr. vs. V.R. Muthara Malingam (1980) 129 ITR 675 (Mad) and also by Patna High Court in the case of ITO vs. East India Coal Co. Ltd. & Ors. (1983) 139 ITR 450 (Pat). The taxpayer must be vigilent to see that once tax in deducted, the same is deposited if not in time but atleast before the prosecution proceedings are initiated.

(iv) For prosecution proceedings also, as directed by CBDT, the show-cause notice is normally issued on such person. After obtaining sanction from Commissioner of Income-tax, Chief Commissioner of Income-tax or Director General, complaint is filed in Criminal Court; the case is heard by Magistrate, who proceeds to frame charges if he is satisfied about the sufficiency of the complaint.

Otherwise he may discharge the person. Just like interest and penalty, there is no time-limit for filing such prosecution also. But again this should be done within a reasonable time as held in Bee Gee Motors & Tractors & Anr. vs. ITO (1995) 218 ITR 155 (P&H).

(v) In case of prosecution the remedy available is to obtain a stay from the High Court. Otherwise the accused could seek discharge by proper representation. Only in case where there is a total violation of natural justice, or if the assessee feels that prosecution filed is mala fide or vexatious or lacks jurisdiction, then only writ in the High Court under Article 226 of the Constitution can be filed.

(vi) Like in other prosecution proceedings, compounding of offence is possible. For this new guidelines have been issued by CBDT recently and the main conditions are:

(a) There must be written request from the assessee;

(b) undisputed tax along with interest and penalty should have been paid; and

(c) assessee should be willing to pay prescribed compounding fees including establishment expenses. On receiving such application of compounding, the Commissioner of Income Tax, Chief Commissioner of Income-tax or Director General or Board can compound the offences by recovery compounding fees collected at fixed percentage, which is at present 5% of the amount which is in default in every month. These are also subject to certain guidelines and upper limit of compounding charges not exceeding Rs. 10 lakhs. These guidelines have been further liberalized.

1.27 Levy of Penal Interest for Default in TDS – Is it mandatory?

Conflicting views have been expressed by the Courts with respect to the chargeability of interest under Section 201(1A) of the Income-tax Act, 1961 for the default in deducting the tax at source or paying the deducted amount to the credit of the Central Government within the prescribed time, especially in a case where the recipient of income has already paid his share of tax liability. It is indeed very ironical that the device of tax deducted at source (TDS) which is, of late, found to be most viable mode of tax-recovery is being riddled with doubts and controversies. The two extreme views have been expressed by the Courts with respect to the chargeability of interest under Section 201(1A) of the Income-tax Act, 1961 for the default in deducting the tax at source or paying the deducted amount to the credit of the Central Government within the prescribed time, especially in a case where the recipient of income has already paid his share of tax liability, simply substantiate the remark.

Chapter XVII of the Income-tax Act deals with the typical mode of tax recovery which is popularly known as TDS, that is, tax deducted at source.

Sections 192 to 196D specify the persons who are mandatory required to deduct the tax at the prescribed rate at the time of making the specified payment to the payee. For instance, Section 192 imposes such a liability on an employer. The tax so deducted or collected has to be paid to the credit of the Central Government within the prescribed time. (Section 200). Failure to deduct tax at source or to pay tax so collected within the specified time exposes the defaulter-assessee to adverse consequences.

One of the consequences, which the defaulter-assessee has to face is liability to penal interest under Section 201(1A) of the Income-tax Act.

Sub-Section (1A) to Section 201 simply provides that if a person fails to deduct the whole or any part of the tax or after deducting fails to pay the tax... "he shall be liable to pay simple interest at twelve per cent per annum (fifteen per cent per annum up to 8th September, 2003 on the amount of such tax from the date on which such tax was deductible to the date on which such tax is actually paid.

Does the specific use of the term "shall" in contradiction to the terms "may", "will" and the like make the levy mandatory in the sense that the moment the specified default is committed the defaulter shall automatically become liable to the interest under Section 201(1A), of course, notwithstanding the fact that the amount in question is recoverable from the defaulter himself/itself? An analysis of the relevant case law reveals that the Bombay, Rajasthan and the Kerala High Courts, respectively, have expressed the view that the use of the word "shall" in Section 201(1A) makes the liability to pay interest mandatory. Neither the existence of any "reasonable cause" (justifying the default) nor the recoverability of the impugned amount from the defaulter or even the receipt of the income could absolve the defaulter from liability to pay interest under Section 201(1A). It is not possible for the Assessing Officer or any of his administrative superiors to waive interest. If there is default, levy of interest is automatic. This is so because such a provision is not a claim for any tax, but is a procedural matter providing machinery for recovery of tax which is compensatory in nature [See Bennet Coleman & Co. Ltd. vs. V.P. Dalme, ITO (1986) 157 ITR 812 (Bom) Pentagon Engineering Pvt. Ltd. vs. CIT (1995) 212 ITR 92 (Bom) CIT vs. Rathi Gum Industries (1995) 213 ITR 98 (Raj) : and CIT vs. Dhanalakshmy Weaving Works: (2000) 245 ITR 13 (Ker) following Sainik Motors vs. State of Rajasthan AIR 1961 SC 1480, Karimtharuvi Tea Estate Ltd. vs. State of Kerala (1960) 66 ITR 262 (SC), CST vs. Qureshi Crucible Centre (1993) 89 STC 467 (SC) and Prahlad Rai vs. STO (1992) 84 STC 375 (SC)].

The hitherto judicially settled mandatory nature of the interest levied under Section 201(1A) of the Act seems to have rather been cracked by the Calcutta High Court in the recent case of West Bengal State Electricity Board 2001 165 CTR(Mad) 502.

In this case, the Calcutta High Court, accepting the assessee's argument, viz, in view of the fact that an appeal lies under Section 246(1)(i) [at present 246A(1)(ha)] against an order imposing interest under Section 201(1A), the word "shall" cannot be mandatory, otherwise the appellate provision will be, partly at least, useless, virtually held that the question whether the levy of interest under Section 201(1A) is mandatory is a substantial question of law and appeal under Section 260A is maintainable.

The logic which fascinated the Calcutta High Court in West Bengal State Electricity Board's case (supra) is logically convincing. For, it must not be forgotten that no independent appeal lies against an order levying penal interest for non/late filing of return and default in the payment/deferment of advance tax, ordained by Sections 234A, 234B and 234C, respectively. It is because of this very reason that the mandatory nature of the said levy continues to be indisputable.

The exact connotation of the term "shall", used in the various provisions of the Act is quite uncertain. It has yet to be decided whether it conveys a mandatory or discretionary nature of the matter concerned. Even the apex Court in Sainik Motors' case (supra) washed its hands by holding that the term "shall" has to be construed in the light of the context of the subject-matter and scope of the relevant statute. And this legal ambiguity over the construction of a crucial term seems to have created frequent mischiefs. The latest being a budding controversy with respect to the mandatory nature of interest for default in deducting or paying tax at source as sought to be levied by Section 201(1A).

In the fitness of the matter, it is, therefore, submitted that the nature of levy ordained by Section 201(1A) be clarified statutorily so that any unnecessary and unwanted controversy could be avoided well in time.

2. COMPLIANCE OF PROVISIONS OF TAX COLLECTION AT SOURCE

2.1 Introduction

The recent amendment to the provisions of Section 206C providing for tax collection at source has created a lot of controversy and practical difficulties. The provisions of tax collection at source were originally introduced by the Finance Act, 1988 with effect from 1st June, 1988. These provisions were initially made applicable to the business of trading in alcoholic liquor and forest produce and the reason given for the same was "Considerable difficulty has been felt in the past in assessing the income of persons who take contract for sale of liquor, forest produce etc. It has been the Department's experience that for taking such contracts, firms or association of persons are specifically constituted and very often no trace is left of them or their members after the contract has been executed. Persons have also been found to have taken contracts in benami names by floating undertakings or associations for short periods. Since tax is payable in the asstt. years on the income of the previous years, the time by which thc income from such sources become assessable , such persons become untraceable. Moreover, at the time of assessment in these cases, either the accounts are not available or they are mostly incorrect or incomplete. Thus, even if assessment could be made on ex parte basis, it becomes almost impossible to collect the tax found due, either because it becomes difficult to establish the identity of the persons and trace them or because of the fact that the persons in whose names contracts were taken are men of no means". (Circular No. 525 dated 24th November, 1988)

It was with the above purpose that a presumptive taxation was made applicable to these businesses under Section 44AC of the Act and collection of tax at source was made applicable on these items under Section 206C. The scope of these provisions was very limited as the definition of the buyer excluded a public sector company, a buyer in the further sale of such goods obtained in pursuance of such sale and a buyer where the goods are not obtained by him by way of auction and whereby the sale price of such goods to be sold by the buyer is fixed under any state act. Though within the meaning of the buyer 'sale by any other mode' of the goods specified was included, still the exclusion of those buyers which do not obtain by way of auction, has limited the application of this provision to sale by way of auction only.

2.2 Amendment by Finance Act, 2003

Provisions of Section 206C – Tax Collection at Source – have been amended from time to time. However, the Finance Act, 2003 has made radical changes. The initial proposal in the Finance Bill, 2003 introduced on 28th February,

2003 was to extend the applicability of this provision to Indian made foreign liquor (IMFL) and Scrap. However, at the time of the final passage of the Bill, the proposal was further amended whereby the scope was further enlarged. The recent amendment to the provisions of Section 206C by the Taxation Laws (Amendment) Ordinance, 2003, though has reduced the rates, but has not addressed many issues on tax collection at source.

As per the amended provisions now every seller is required to collect tax from the buyer in respect of the following goods at the rate specified against each item.

i)	Alcoholic liquor for human consumption	1%
ii)	Tendu leaves	5%
iii)	Timber obtained under forest leaves	2.5%
iv)	Timber obtained by any mode other than under the forest leaves	2.5%
v)	Any other forest produce not being timber or tendu leaves	2.5%
vi)	Scrap	1%

The definition of the seller has been expanded by the Finance Act, 2003 and it shall include all persons including individual and Hindu Undivided Family whose sales/receipts in the immediately preceding financial year exceeded the amount specified under Section 44AB of the Act. The definition of the buyer has also been amended. Buyer now means a person who obtain such goods by way of auction, tender or <u>any other mode</u> but does not include

i) a public sector company, the central, state govt., embassy, foreign state and club

ii) a buyer in the retail sale of such goods for pursual consumption.

The above definition of the buyer is very exhaustive as it includes sales by 'any other mode' and excludes only a buyer in the retail trade, i.e., a person who buys in the retail for his own use and accordingly does not exclude trader.

The definition of scrap has also been inserted in the explanation. Scrap has been defined to mean waste and scrap from the manufacture or mechanical working of material which is definitely not usable as such because of breakage, cutting up, wear, other reasons.

2.3 Scope of amended provisions

With the amendment in the definition of the buyer now every person who sells goods specified above to any buyer is required to collect tax at source at the rate specified above. The only exception shall be when the goods are sold in a retail trade for personal purposes. This will not mean that the retail trader is not covered. Exclusion is of a retail buyer, not the retail trader. As these provisions are applicable to 'timber' whether obtained under forest lease or by any other mode, all persons who are selling 'timber' except to a retail buyer are now required to collect tax at source @ 2.5 percent. The application of this provision will be on all importers, wholesales, distributors of 'timber' at every stage of sale. It is not one time levy. The purpose of the Section is to collect tax at source on the income of the persons to whom goods are being sold.

Similarly in the case of scrap, the liability to collect tax at source will be on every seller except when the sale is being made to manufacturers. In that case a declaration on the prescribed form will be required. There is nothing in the provision to suggest that it is only applicable on scrap arising from the manufacture or mechanical working of materials within India. Accordingly the liability to collect tax will be even on imported scrap and as in the case of timber will be applicable to importers, wholesalers, distributors etc. The scrap however, will not include by-products. The definition of scrap has been restricted and means waste and scrap from the manufacture or mechanical working of materials and which is definitely not usable as such, because of breakage, cutting up, wear and other reasons. In view of the above definition, the provisions shall be applicable to only that scrap or waste which fulfills the following conditions.

i) It arises from manufacture or mechanical working of materials; and
ii) It is not definitely usable as such because of breakage, cutting up, wear and other reasons,

Both the above conditions should be satisfied for making the provisions applicable in the case of scrap. In view of the above interpretation, newspaper, ruddi, empty bottles, sacks etc may not fall within the meaning of scrap. Similarly bagasse and molasses of sugar mills may not fall within the definition of scrap as it is usable in the same shape.

2.4 Rates not commensurate with the profit

The applicability of these provisions and tax rate of 2.5 percent on Timber had made the sale of timber in the market almost impossible. A tax of Rs.2.5 percent on the sale of Rs.100 is possible only when there is a net profit margin of 8.33 percent and that too when the buyer falls in the maximum tax rate slab of 30 percent. This means that the buyer who buys the timber of Rs.100 is able to sell the same at Rs.115 and after meeting overheads of say Rs.6.67 earns a net income of Rs.8.33. Only then there can be tax liability of Rs.2.50. A net margin of 8.33 percent in the wholesale trade of timber is almost impossible. It is to be noted that retailer of timber by and large makes sale of timber to consumer for personal consumption and will not be required to collect tax at source.

Such a high margin and that too in the wholesale trade is not possible. It appears that at the time of drafting of these amendments the ground realities of the timber trade have again been ignored.

The provision of this Section has also been extended to IMFL and the tax @ 1 percent is to be collected on the sale of IMFL. It appears that the Association of Indian Made Foreign Liquor was able to persuade the government to reduce the tax to one per cent. Probably the businessmen in the trade of timber are not so better organized as those in the trade of IMFL. Otherwise there is no reason why the rate of 1 per cent should not have been applied to timber also. The net margin in the trading of IMFL/Country Liquor is definitely more than in the timber trade. Dealers of timber trade particularly of imported timber operate on very thin margin and chances of income escaping tax net is also very low as compared to those in the trade of country liquor/IMFL.

2.5 Widening of scope to all sales not justified

As stated in the beginning, the purpose of introducing the scheme of tax collection at source was only to get hold of those persons who take contracts for sale of liquor, forest produce etc and thereafter become untraceable. The objective of introducing the scheme of tax collection at source was not to collect tax at source of importers, wholesalers, and distributors etc who have their organized businesses and can be easily traced as all transactions by and large are through banking channels. The intention of the present legislation also does not appear to be to include these types of transactions. But a last minute amendment in the Act without any explanation has created a chaotic situation. Either there should be a categorical declaration by the government that it wants to change the objective of tax collection at source as stated in the Circular No. 525 dated 24th November, 1988 and introduce a new system of collection of tax at source and which shall be applicable to not only sale by way of auction, tender etc but all sales. And if that be so, why it should then be restricted to the trade of timber, scrap, liquor, forest produce only, why not to all other items such as cement, steel, chemicals etc. If that is not the intention of making this amendment, then only those sales which arise by way of auction or tender should be covered and all other sales should be excluded.

2.6 Strict interpretation of definition of buyer includes sale by way of auction, tender etc., not all sales

A plain reading of the amended definition of the buyer given in Clause (a) of Explanation suggests that any sale by way of auction, tender and '<u>by any other mode</u>' will be covered. However, if we have a close look at this definition of the buyer, then one interpretation can be that only those sales which are in the nature of auction, tender shall be covered, not all sales. This is because the words "by any other mode" have to get their meaning from the preceding words, i.e., auction and tender following the rule of *ejusdem generis*. If the meaning of words 'any other mode' was to include all sales, then there was no need to specify sale by way of auction and tender. This interpretation also gets supported from the objective of introducing Section 206C

2.7 Compliance of Provisions of Section 206C

Despite the various difficulties stated above law is law and that being in force, now every person liable to collect tax at source under the provisions of Section 206C is required to comply with the various requirements as explained below:

(a) Tax Collection Account Number

Every person who is selling any of the goods specified in Section 206C is required to apply and obtain a new number called Tax Collection Account Number (TCAN) under Section 206CA. This number is to be obtained in addition to PAN, applicable to all taxpayers and Tax Deduction at Source Number (TAN), applicable to all who are liable to deduct tax at source. Application for allotment, however, is to be made in Form No. 49B i.e., the same form which is used for obtaining TDS No., within one month from the end of the month in which tax is collected. The penalty for default in applying TCAN is Rs. Ten thousand under Section 272BBB of the Act.

(b) Deposit of Tax

A seller who is required to collect tax at source is under an obligation to collect this tax

i) at the time of debit to the buyer; or

ii) receipt of such amount from the buyer in cash or cheque or draft; or

iii) by any other mode.

whichever is earlier.

This amount so collected is to be deposited with the government within the time to be prescribed. This period prescribed by Rules is within 7 days from the end of the month in which it is collected/debited. Even if the goods are sold on credit and the payments have not been received from the buyers, the seller is required to deposit the amount of tax collection out of his own sources. In case a seller fails to collect tax or after collecting tax fails to deposit the same, he is liable to pay interest @ 12 percent p.a.(Reduced from 15 per cent with effect from 8.9.2003) from the date on which such tax was collectible to the date the tax is actually paid under Section 206C(7) of the Act..

(c) Issue of Certificate

The seller is required to issue certificate of collection of tax at source within the period prescribed. Earlier the period prescribed was 10 days. The new period prescribed by Rules is one month from the end of the month in which TCS is debited or collected. However, at the request of the concerned person, consolidated certificate for six months ended 30th September and 31st March respectively, can be issued within one month from the end of the relevant six month. Even if the buyer has not made payment to the seller, as is usual in the case of credit sale, the seller has to issue certificate to the buyer of the tax collected at source. The penalty for failure to issue the certificate is Rs. one hundred for every day of default under Section 272A(2)(g) of the Act.

(d) Filing of Return

The seller is required to file half-yearly returns, i.e., 30th September and 31st March as against yearly returns in the case of tax deduction at source within one month from the end of the half year. Return is to be filed in form No.27E as amended by notification dt. 31st July,2003. Now there is only one consolidated return form for all types of collection on sale of scrap, timber, IMFL etc. Penalty for failure to file the return is Rs. one hundred per day but shall not exceed the amount of tax collectible under Section 272A(2)(c) of the Act. The TCS on scrap, IMFL etc. has come into operation from 8th September, 2003. Accordingly, the first return for the six months ended 30th September, 2003 is due on 31st October, 2003.

(e) Exemption from levy of tax collection at source

For those buyers who want to buy the goods specified for the purpose of manufacturing, processing, producing articles or things and not for trading purposes, the provisions of tax collection at source are not applicable, in case they submit a declaration form in the prescribed Form 27C in duplicate to the seller. Copy of this form is to be submitted by the seller to the Commissioner within 7 days from the end of the month in which such form is received. It is to be noted that the Board vide its letter dt. 22nd June, 1988 addressed to Nagpur Timber Merchants Association has clarified that round timber processed and cut into various sizes as per orders from different markets will amount to processing and no tax is to be collected at source from saw mill owners in such cases.

(f) Issue of Certificate of a lower rate

Tax collection at source is to be made from the buyer by the seller at the prescribed rate. However, in case any buyer justifies that tax collection in his case should be at a rate lower than the prescribed rate, then the Assessing Officer shall issue a certificate of lower rate on application being made in the prescribed Form No. 13 (Substituted for form no.27F with effect from 1.10.2003) by the buyer. As explained above, the prescribed tax rates particularly for timber trade is too high and tax collection at source at a rate lower than the prescribed rate will be justified in all the cases. Administratively it will be difficult both for all these buyers to apply the certificate and for the department to handle such large number of applications.

(g) Exemption

Sale to public sector company, central, state government, embassy and to a club, however is exempt from the provisions of Section 206C. As such liquor seller need not collect tax at source on supply to a club.

3. SUGGESTIONS FOR RATIONALISATION OF PROCEDURES

Introduction

As stated in the beginning the provisions of TDS over the period have become complicated and administratively difficult to handle by the tax deductor as well as the tax authorities. Given below are some of the suggestion which can help in the simplification as well as better administration both for the tax deductor and the tax authorities.

3.1 Procedure should enhance compliance rather than defiance

Presently TDS provisions are such that the tax deductor despite his best intention to comply with the TDS provisions have difficulties in complying with the same because of delay or default as there is no remedy available under the Act once there is a delay or default. As such, once a delay and default has taken place, the tax deductor is left with no option but just to ignore the compliance. The income tax department is not always able to deduct such cases and then to follow it up by levying interest and penalty. The *suo motto* compliance will always be better and more efficient as against at the initiative of the department. Presently if a tax deductor has failed to deduct or deducted less amount, the revenue can recover the tax amount if the deductee has not paid tax on the income. Further, interest can also be recovered. However, if the deductor has filed its return and later comes across a mistake he has no way out. It is suggested that for promoting compliance the tax deductor be authorized to contact the deductee and in case he has not made payment of the taxes on the income subject to deduction then deduct the tax at source at that point of time and make the payment along with interest and issue the certificate to the deductee. In case the deductee has made the payment then the deductor should obtain evidence of the payment and deposit the interest for the delay and file the necessary documents to the department on the prescribed proforma. This will ensure that income subject to deduction of tax at source does not go untaxed.

3.2 Procedure for verification of TDS Return

TDS returns are filed under Section 206 of the Income Tax with the Assessing Officer TDS Ward as he is the designated officer under Rule 36A of Income Tax Rules, 1962. Section 206 places on obligation on the person responsible for deducting tax, to prepare and deliver TDS returns to the designated officer as prescribed. Various TDS returns have been prescribed under Rule 36, 36A, 37, 37A and 37B. The present Act and Rules nowhere prescribes any procedure and mode for the verification of TDS returns furnished by the person responsible for deducting tax.

However notices are issued by Assessing Officers whereby information is being asked for on various matters for verification of TDS return. These notices are general and ask for a lot of information including books of accounts as is usually asked in the case of a scrutiny assessment under Section 143(2) of the Act. No Section is being quoted in these notices under which this information is being asked for. However, in case of non-compliance of the above said notice, another letter is being forwarded by the TDS Officers where it is stated that information is being called for under Section 133(6). Section 133(6) gives power to the Assessing Officer to call for the information where any proceeding is pending before him. Since no proceeding is pending before the TDS Officer, Section 133(6) cannot be invoked. Further, Section 133(6) can not be invoked in a routine manner for verification of TDS returns. Some of the notices are issued under Section 131. Section 131 gives power to the Assessing Officer to issue summon just as a court has power while trying a suit. This being the case , the TDS Officer can issue summon under Section 131 only when a proceeding is pending before him. A court has power to issue summon when a suit is being tried before it under Code of Civil Procedure i.e. when proceedings are before it. It is an admitted fact that at the time when notice under Section 131 is issued by the TDS Officer, no proceedings are pending before him.

For verification of income tax returns filed under Section 139 and under Section 142(1) (not TDS return), power has been given to the Assessing Officer under Sections 142(1) and 143(2) of the Act. These two Sections prescribes the mode and method in which income tax returns can be verified by the Assessing Officer. No such procedure and mode has been prescribed for verification of TDS returns. It appears that at the time of the enactment the TDS functions were supposed to be a part of the Assessing Officer dealing with income tax returns. However, later on separate TDS Officers were designated to handle TDS matters but without providing any procedure and mode of verification of TDS returns. There is no Section in the Income Tax Act under which a notice can be issued for verification of TDS return. In the absence of any specific provision under the Act, verification of TDS returns by issuing a letter calling the records of the assessee, books of accounts etc. is not in accordance with the provisions of the Act. It is suggested that procedure for verification of returns be streamlined by making a statutory provision like Section 143(2) (limited scrutiny), prescribing time within which notice can be issued, the time period in which proceedings are to be completed and also time and procedure for cases where income has escaped tax deduction at source on the line of Section 147 and Section 153.

3.3 <u>Time limit for verification of TDS returns</u>

At present there is no time limit for completion of asstt of TDS return filed by the assessee. The TDS officer can call for record of any years. Provision should be introduced on the line of Section 153, to provide for time limit of TDS matters. This can be 2 years from the end of the relevant financial year.

3.4 Issue of TDS Certificate be linked with date of payment.

Presently payment of tax deducted and issue of TDS Certificate both are linked to the due date of deduction of tax at source. Delay in payment of tax deducted at source is subjected to penal interest under Section 201(1A) of the Act, whereas delay in issue of TDS Certificate is subjected to penalty of Rs. 100/- per day for each certificate under Section 272A(2)(g) of the Act.

With so many transaction being subjected to TDS provisions, there is every likelihood that in some of the cases, there is error/omission of deduction of tax at source, which is pointed out later on by the auditors or detected during inspection or checking done internally by the assessee. As such, issue of TDS Certificate, which is linked, with the due date of deduction of tax at source causes a lot of hardship. This provision of issue of TDS certificate be de-linked with the due date of deduction of tax at source and be linked with the actual date of payment of TDS. It will also meet the requirement of TDS Certificate i.e. Forms 16 and 16A where details of payment of tax in Govt. Treasury have to be stated.

Further as per the provisions of the Act and the rules, TDS Certificates can be issued even in those cases where the payment have not been made by the deductor. There is no explicit provision whereby deductor is prohibited from issuing TDS Certificate unless the payment of the tax deducted as indicated in the certificate has been made. This sometimes may lead to evasion of tax by the deductor who may not make the payment of tax after issue of the certificate but the deductee on the basis of the certificate may get the credit. It is very difficult for the Assessing Officer to verify each and every TDS certificate and even legally to withhold tax credit on the basis of TDS certificate in which details of the payment are not stated. It is suggested that there should be an explicit provision that no TDS certificate can be issued by the deductor unless full payment of the tax stated in the certificate has been made and the details of the same are given in the certificate. A corresponding amendment will be required whereby issue of TDS certificate has to be linked with the date of payment. One option can be to amend the rule and to provide for that TDS certificate will be issued within 7 days from the end of the month in which the tax is deposited with no reference to the date when the TDS has accrued or deducted. This will also avoid the tendency on the part of the tax deductor to backdate TDS certificate to avoid penal provision.

3.5 Consolidated return of tax deduction at source

Presently different returns have to be filed by every taxpayer who is liable for tax deduction at source for different types of payments. It is suggested that a consolidated return be prescribed for TDS. There should be different pages for various types of payments liable for tax deduction at source as is in the case of return of income where income has to be computed under different heads and then tax is computed on the aggregate amount. This will avoid a lot of paper work and the handling and verification of return will also become easy with the department. This suggestion has since been accepted by the CBDT. Now there is a consolidated return Form No.26 for various types of tax deducted.

3.6 Consolidated challan for every month

Presently for each type of payment separate challan has to be filled in every month. This increases the workload not only with the tax deductor but also with the bank and the Income Tax Department. It is suggested that a consolidated challan for all types of payments be prescribed. The deductor should deposit all the tax which he has deducted during the month for various types of payments under a single challan. As such there will be only 12 challans with a consolidated return.

3.7 Certification of TDS return

With the increase in the number of returns and the workload with the Income Tax Department it is almost practically impossible to verify all returns. As such to ensure that the TDS returns filed by the tax deductor are correct it is suggested that the TDS returns be audited and verified by a Chartered Accountant in the case of those tax deductors who are depositing TDS beyond a prescribed amount.

3.8 Revision of TDS returns

Presently there is no provision for revising the TDS return with the result that any mistake/omission detected by the assessee can not be rectified. In most of the cases during the course of tax audit which is usually conducted during the month of September, October, the tax auditors come across cases where tax is required to be deducted but has not been detected or short deducted. In all such cases the assessee shows its inability to deduct tax as he has already filed the TDS return and moreover the person whose tax is to be deducted may have also filed his return of income without claim of the said TDS deductable but not deducted. To take care of this type of situation it is suggested that provision for revising TDS return be introduced. As a deterrent, the assessee besides paying interest under Section 201(1A) of the Act for delayed payment of TDS be asked to pay interest (just like Section 234A of the Act) @ 1.00 per cent per month on the amount of TDS. Correspondingly credit for TDS certificate issued late in such cases be allowed by way of rectification under Section 154 of the Act, where the assessee whose tax has been deducted and has filed the return without claim of such TDS certificates in case the TDS certificate has been received by him after the date of filing his return of income. With the introduction of Section 155(14) allowing credit of TDS certificates filed within a period of 2 years from the end of asstt year, legally there should not be any problem. This will go a long way in increasing the collection of TDS, as all errors, omissions pointed out by the tax auditors will be rectified by the assessee. The revenue will be suitably compensated by way of normal interest under Section 201(IA) like 234B as well as deterrent interest like 234A.

3.9 <u>Interest under Section 201(1A) be paid suo–motto.</u>

Presently under Section 201(1A) interest is leviable on late payment of TDS. This interest is not payable on self asstt basis but a demand has to be created by the ITO (TDS) after processing the TDS returns. With the increase in work load of TDS returns, it is not possible for ITO (TDS) to verify each and every TDS return and compute interest under Section 201(1A) of the Act. It is suggested that interest payable under Section 201(1A) should be on self asstt basis and be paid before filing TDS return and challan be enclosed with TDS return. This will increase the collection and voluntary compliance.

3.10 <u>Interest on late payment of tax</u>

Presently interest on refund, if any, is allowed on the tax deducted with effect from 1st April despite the fact that the tax has been deposited by the tax deductor on 31st May. There is no provision at present to link the payment of interest on the refund with the date of the payment of tax by the tax deductor. In some cases the tax is deducted at source as early as in April of the previous year where as in other cases the tax is paid as late as two months after the end of the previous year. As against this liability to pay advance tax arises in the month of September, December and March of the previous year. In such a situation, the deductee loses interest on early deduction and payment and gains interest on late deduction and payment. It is suggested that the provision be modified to make the same equitable so that neither the revenue loses money nor the deductee.

3.11 <u>Penalty for late issue of certificate when the deductor fails to produce certificate from deductee.</u>

No penalty be levied for late issue of TDS certificate in case the assessee produces a certificate from the concerned person that he has not been effected or prejudiced by late issue of certificate as is required for issuing consolidated certificate for a year as against obligation to issue individual certificate.

3.12 <u>Penalty should have nexus with the amount in default</u>

Presently penalty at the rate of Rs.100 per day for delay in issuing TDS certificate is leviable. The amount of Rs.100 per day has no nexus with the amount involved and the number of TDS certificate. In all fairness penalty for late issue of certificate be linked with the amount of tax involved and as such penalty for late issue of TDS Certificate and late filing of TDS return should also be @ 1.00 per cent per month of the amount of tax covered by the TDS certificate or the TDS return in the shape of interest and be payable on self asstt. basis.

3.13 Procedure for lower deduction of tax at source

Presently under Section 197 any person whose income is liable for tax deduction at source desires that the tax be deducted at a rate lower than the prescribed rate he has to make an application to the TDS Officer. His application is required to be made at the prescribed Form No. 13. The information required in Form No. 13 is not very clear and as such there is a wide discretion rather arbitrariness available to the Assessing Officer while issuing certificate for lower deduction of tax. The purpose of deduction of tax at source is to ensure that tax is paid by all those who have income liable to tax. The purpose of tax deduction at source is not to collect higher rate initially and then refund the tax. The rate of tax prescribed for deduction of tax at source for various incomes is only indicative rate. With the applicability of TDS provisions for large number of payments the number of persons seeking certificate of lower deduction of tax at source has increased over the period. As such to avoid inconvenience and harassment to these persons it is desired that the procedure for the issue of certificate for lower deduction be streamlined. The applicant be asked to submit particulars of income for the last three years and the tax payable thereon. The applicant also be asked to submit the details of total receipts under the various heads which are liable for deduction of tax at source. The projected figures for the current year should also be stated in the application and the rate of tax should be worked out on the basis of these projections. The TDS officer should accept the figures stated in the application and in case he has any objection then he has to state reasons and should pass a speaking order if he wants to enhance the rate of tax for deduction at source. A time frame of may be 15 days or one month should be prescribed for issue of certificate by the TDS Officer. If need be the application may also be certified by a Chartered Accountant so that the figures stated for the preceding year need not be verified by the department. As a crosscheck a column should be provided in the application to provide details of certificate obtained in the earlier years and the comparison with the tax rate at which the certificate was issued and the tax rate which ultimately comes to on the basis of returned income may also be provided. This can discourage the assessee of giving wrong projections of the current year.

3.14 Failure of Deductor to issue TDS Certificate to Deductee

Presently under the Act there is no method by which a deductee can approach the department in case he doesn't get the TDS Certificate within the prescribed period. The only remedy available to him under the Act is under Section 205 where demand against him can not be enforced. In case where there is a refund then the deductee has no option and can not take the help of the department in getting the TDS Certificate. The non-issue of TDS Certificate to the deductee is by and large on account of non-payment of tax deducted at source by the deductor and the department either never comes to know of this fact or it comes to the notice of the department very late when the assessee invokes the provision of Section 205 at the time of recovery of the demand. It is suggested that a suitable provision be introduced either under Section 203 or under Section 205 making it obligatory on the deductee to inform the department in the prescribed proforma giving the name, address, particulars, nature of income, amount of income, tax deducted at source within a period of say 30 days from the date of filing the return. This information should be submitted with the Commissioner of Income Tax like Form 15G being submitted presently or this can be given to the Commissioner (TDS). Thereafter the Commissioner (TDS) can follow up the matter with the tax deductor and ensure the payment of tax deducted at source and also ensure the issue of TDS Certificate to the tax deductee. This will facilitate the recovery of tax which otherwise goes unnoticed and will also help the tax deductee in getting credit of the tax deducted at source.

3.15 <u>Rates for tax deduction be specified for all types of income for non-residents</u>

Presently under Section 195 rates for tax deduction are prescribed for certain types of income only. For other types of income, no such rates are prescribed and tax has to be deducted on the gross income unless the non-resident deductee approaches the A.O. for lower deduction of tax. It is suggested that rates for tax deduction be prescribed for each type of income after analyzing the expected tax liability, so that every non-resident is not required to approach the A.O. for certificate of lower deduction.

4. IMPORTANT CIRCULARS AND CLARIFICATIONS

4.1 Circular No.719 of 22nd August 1995
Returns under Section 206 - TDS - Clarification
F.No. 275/206/95-IT(B)

Subject: Filing of returns under Section 206 of the Income-tax Act, 1961, in respect of tax deducted at source from the salary of employees of a company working at its headquarters or in other branches - Clarification regarding.

1. Under Section 204(i) of the Income-tax Act, 1961, where salary is paid by a company, the person responsible for deducting tax at source under Section 192 is the company itself, including the principal officer thereof. The principal officer is defined under Section 2(35) of the Act.

2. In some cases, tax in respect of all the employees of the company is being deducted at source at the Head Office and the return under Section 206 is filed at the place where the HO is situated. In some other cases, the companies are discharging this responsibility partly through their branch offices requiring the company to file the return with them even where this is being filed with the Assessing Officer where branch or Head Office is situated.

3. It is clarified that where the Head Office or the branch office is already filing the return under Section 206 no other Assessing Officer shall require the assessee to file such return with him. Where, however, the return is not being filed, the Assessing Officer having jurisdiction in terms of Rule 36A of Income-tax Rules may proceed so as to enforce compliance to the provisions relating to deduction of tax at source from 'Salary'.

(Sd.)
Anjani Kumar,
Director (Budget).
[F.No. 275/206/95-IT(B)]

4.2 TDS returns Can be filed at Head office
Circular No.744 of 6th May, 1996
TDS - Salaries Return under Section 206

Filing of returns under Section 206 of Income-tax Act, 1961, in respect of tax deducted at source from the salary of employees of a company working at its headquarters or in other branches - Extension of the procedure in respect of TDS returns - Clarification regarding.

Board's Circular No.719 (F.No.275/206/95-IT(B), dated 22nd August, 1995, states that where the head office or the branch office is already filing the returns under Section 206, no other Assessing Officer shall require the assessee to file such return with him. Where, however, the return is not being filed, the Assessing Officer having jurisdiction in terms of rule 36A of the Income–Tax Rules, may proceed so as to enforce compliance to the provisions relating to deduction of tax at source from "salary."

It has been decided to extend this procedure to all other TDS returns filed under rule 37, as required under Section 206 of the Income–Tax Act, 1961.

(Sd) Y.P. Vashishat,
Under Secretary Budget
[F.No.275/34/96-IT(B)]

4.3 Circular No.715 of 8th August 1995 TDS - Finance Act, 1995 - FAQ

Subject: Clarification on various provisions relating to tax deducted at source-Regarding.

The Finance Act, 1995, has enlarged the scope of income-tax deduction at source by making various amendments. In regard to the changes introduced through the Finance Act, 1995, a number of queries have been received from the various associations and professional bodies on the scope of tax deduction at source. It would be desirable to clarify the doubts by issuing a public circular in the form of question answers as under:

Question 1: What would be the scope of an advertising contract for purpose of Section 194C of the Act?
Answer: The term 'advertising' has not been defined in the Act. During the course of the consideration of the Finance Bill, 1995, the Finance Minister clarified on the floor of the House that the amended provisions of tax deduction at source would apply when a client makes payment to an advertising agency and not when advertising agency makes payment to the media, which includes both print and electronic media. The deduction is required to be made at the rate of 1 per cent. It was further clarified that when an advertising agency makes payments to their models, artists, photographers, etc., the tax shall be deducted at the rate of 5 per cent as applicable to fees for professional and technical services under Section 194J of the Act.

Question 2: Whether the advertising agency would deduct tax at source out of payments made to the media?
Answer: No. The position has been clarified in the answer to question No.1 above.

Question 3: At what rate is tax to be deducted if the advertising agencies give a consolidated bill including charges for art work and other related jobs as well as payments made by them to media?

Answer: The deduction will have to be made under Section 194C at the rate of 1 per cent. The advertising agencies shall have to deduct tax at source at the rate of 5 per cent under Section 194J while making payments to artists, actors, models, etc. If payments are made for production of programmes for the purpose of broadcasting and telecasting, these payments will be subjected to TDS @ 2 per cent. Even if the production of such programmes is for the purpose of preparing advertisement material, not for immediate advertising, the payment will be subject to TDS at the rate of 2 per cent.

Question 4: Where the tax required to be deducted at source on payments made directly to the print media / Doordarshan for release of advertisements?

Answer: The payments made directly to print and electronic media would be covered under Section 194C as these are in the nature of payments for purposes of advertising. Deduction will have to be made at the rate of 1 per cent. It may, however, be clarified that the payments made directly to Doordarshan may not be subjected to TDS as Doordarshan, being a Government agency, is not liable to income-tax.

Question 5: Whether a contract for putting up a boarding be covered under Section 194C or 194-I of the Act?

Answer: The contract for putting up a hoarding is in the nature of advertising contract and provisions of Section 194C would be applicable. It may, however, be clarified that if a person has taken a particular space on rent and thereafter sub-lets the same fully or in part for putting up a hoarding, he would be liable to TDS under Section 194-I and not 194C of the Act.

Question 6: Whether payment under a contract for carriage of goods or passengers by any mode of transport include payment made to a travel agent for purchase of a ticket or payment made to a clearing and forwarding agent for carriage of goods?

Answer: The payments made to a travel agent an airline for purchase of a ticket for travel would not be subjected to tax deduction at source as the privity of the contract is between the individual passenger and the airline / travel agent, not withstanding the fact that the payment is made by an entity mentioned in Section 194C(1). The provisions of Section 194C shall, however, apply when a plane or a bus or any other mode of transport is chartered by one of the entities mentioned in Section 194C of the Act. As regards payments made to clearing and forwarding agents for carriage of goods, the same shall be subjected to tax deduction at source under Section 194C of the Act.

Question 7: Whether a travel agent / clearing and forwarding agent would be required to deduct tax at source from the sum payable by the agent to an airline or other carrier of goods or passengers?

Answer: The travel agent, issuing tickets on behalf of the airlines for travel of individual passengers, would not be required to deduct tax at source as he acts on behalf of the airlines. The position of clearing and forwarding agents is different. They act as independent contractors. Any payment made to them would, hence, be liable for deduction of tax at source. They would also be liable to deduct tax at source while making payments to a carrier of goods.

Question 8: Whether Section 194C would be attracted in respect of payments made to couriers for carrying documents, letters etc.?

Answer: The carriage of documents, letters etc., is in the nature of carriage of goods and, therefore, provisions of Section 194C would be attracted in respect of payments made to the couriers.

Question 9: In the case of payments to transporters, can each GR be said to be a separate contract, even though payments for several GRs are made under one bill?

Answer : Normally, each GR can be said to be a separate contract, if the goods are transported at one time. But if the goods are transported continuously in pursuance of a contract for a specific period or quantity, each GR will not be a separate contract and all GRs relating to that period or quantity will be aggregated for the purpose of the TDS.

Question 10: Whether there is any obligation to deduct tax at source out of payment of freight when the goods are received on "freight to pay" basis?

Answer: Yes. The provisions of tax deduction at source are applicable irrespective of the actual payment.

Question 11: Whether a contract for catering would include serving food in a restaurant/sale of eatables?

Answer: TDS is not required to be made when payment is made for serving food in a restaurant in the normal, course of running of the restaurant/cafe.

Question 12: Whether payment to a recruitment agency can be covered by Section 194C ?

Answer: Provisions of Section 194C apply to a contract for carrying out any work including supply of labour for carrying out any work. Payment to recruitment agencies are in the nature of payments for services rendered. Accordingly, provisions of Section 194C shall not apply. The payment will, however, be subject to TDS under Section 194J of the Act.

Question 13: Whether Section 194C would cover payments made by a company to a share registrar?

Answer: In view of the answer to the earlier question, such payments will not be liable for tax deduction at source under Section 194C. But these will be liable to tax deduction at source under Section 194J.

Question 14: Whether FD commission and brokerage can be covered under Section 194C?

Answer: No.

Question 15: Whether Section 194C would apply in respect of supply of printed material as per prescribed specifications?

Answer: Yes.

Question 16: Whether tax is required to be deducted at source under Section 194C or 194J on payment of commission to external parties for procuring orders for the company's product?

Answer: Rendering of services for procurement of orders is not covered under the provisions of Section 194C. However, rendering of such services may involve payment of fees for professional or technical services, in which case tax may be deductible under the provisions of Section 194J.

Question 17: Whether advertisement contracts are covered under Section 194C only to the extent of payment of commission to the person who arranges release of advertisement, etc., or whether deduction is to be made on the gross amount including bill of media?

Answer: Tax is to be deducted at the rate of 1 per cent. of the gross amount of the bill.

Question 18: Whether deduction of tax is required to be made under Section 194C for sponsorship of debates, seminars and other functions held in colleges, schools and associations with a view to earn publicity through display of banners, etc., put up by the organisers?

Answer: The agreement of sponsorship is, in essence, an agreement for carrying out a work of advertisement. Therefore, provisions of Section 194C shall apply.

Question 19: Whether deduction of tax is required to be made on payments for cost of advertisements issued in the souvenirs brought out by various organisations?

Answer: Yes.

Question 20: Whether payments made to a hotel for rooms hired during the year would be of the nature of rent ?

Answer: Payments made by persons other than individuals and HUFs for hotel accommodation taken on regular basis will be in the nature of rent subject to TDS under Section 194-I.

Question 21: Whether the limit of Rs.1,20,000 per annum would apply separately for each co-owner of a property?

Answer: Under Section 194-I, the tax is deductible from payment by way of rent, if such payment to the payee during the year is likely to be Rs.1,20,000 or more. If there are a number of payees, each having a definite and ascertainable share in the property, the limit of Rs.1,20,000 will apply to each of the payees/co-owners separately. The payers and payees are, however, advised not to enter into sham agreements to avoid TDS provisions.

Question 22: Whether the rent paid should be enhanced for national income in respect of deposit given to the landlord?

Answer: The tax is to be deducted from actual payment and there is no need of computing notional income in respect of a deposit given to the landlord. If the deposit is adjustable against future rent, the deposit is in the nature of advance rent subject to TDS.

Question 23: Whether payments made by company taking premises on rent but styling the agreement as a business centre agreement would attract the provisions of Section 194-I?

Answer: The tax is to be deducted from rent paid, by whatever name called, for hire of a property. The incidence of deduction of tax at source does not depend upon the nomenclature, but on the content of the agreement as mentioned in clause (i) of Explanation to Section 194-I.

Question 24: Whether in a case of composite arrangement for user of premises and provision of manpower for which consideration is paid as a specified percentage of turnover, Section 194-I of the Act would be attracted?

Answer: If the composite arrangement is in essence the agreement for taking premises on rent, the tax will be deducted under Section 194-I from payments thereof.

Question 25: Whether the receipts prior to July 1, 1995, are to be aggregated to determine the limit of Rs.20,000 for each financial year?

Answer: Clause (B) of proviso to Section 194J(1) makes it clear that tax shall be deducted at source if the aggregate sums credited or paid or likely to be credited or paid during the financial year are likely to exceed Rs.20,000. Therefore, in regard to financial year 1995-96, the limit of Rs.20,000 will have to be worked out taking into account all the payments from April 1, 1995 to March 31, 1996. But the deduction of tax at source would be made at the specified rate only from the payment made on or after July 1, 1995.

Question 26: Whether payments made to a hospital for rendering medical services will attract deduction of tax at source under Section 194J?

Answer: Yes.

Question 27: Whether commission received by the advertising agency from the media would require deduction of tax at source under Section 194J of the Act?

Answer: Yes.

Question 28: Whether the services of a regular electrician on contract basis will fall in the ambit of technical services to attract the provisions of Section 194J of the Act? In case the services of the electrician are provided by a contractor, whether the provisions of Section 194C or 194J would be applicable?

Answer: The payments made to an electrician or to a contractor who provides the service of an electrician will be in the nature of payment made in pursuance of a contract for carrying out any work. Accordingly, provisions of Section 194C will apply in such cases.

Question 29: Whether a maintenance contract including supply of spares would be covered under Section 194C or 194J of the Act?
Answer: Routine, normal maintenance contracts which include supply of spares will be covered under Section 194C. However, where technical services are rendered, the provision of Section 194J will apply in regard to tax deduction at source.

Question 30: Whether the deduction of tax at source under Section 194C and 194J has to be made out of the gross amount of the bill including reimbursement or excluding reimbursement for actual expenses?
Answer: Section 194C and 194J refer to any sum paid. Obviously, reimbursements cannot be deducted out of the bill amount for the purpose of tax deduction at source.

Question 31: Whether TDS from income in respect of units is applicable to dividend or is it applicable to capital appreciation distributed at the time of re-purchase / redemption of the units?
Answer: The provisions of Section 194K regarding deduction of tax at source from income in respect of units are applicable to periodical distribution of income, which is in the nature of dividend. These provisions do not apply to capital gains arising at the time of re-purchase or redemption of the units.

Question 32: Whether TDS on reinvestment term deposit should be made on accrual basis, which is quarterly, or once in a financial year?
Answer: Tax has to be deducted at source at the time of credit of interest to the account of the payee or at the time of payment thereof, whichever is earlier. If credit is given to the account of the payee or payment is made to him annually, the tax may be deducted annually. It may be clarified that a credit to interest payable account or suspense account etc., is also taken as credit to the account of the payee, even though this credit is not reflected separately in the payee's account.

Question 33: Whether variable deposit schemes are liable to deduction of tax at source from interest?
Answer: Under Section 194A, tax is to be deducted from interest from banks on time deposits. As variable deposits are in the nature of time deposits, tax is deductible at source from interest on such deposits.

Question 34: Whether tax has to be deducted from principal on renewal of deposits made after July 1, 1995, but which matured on or before June 30, 1995, when the renewal is made retrospectively?
Answer: Tax has to be deducted from interest credited or paid, whichever is earlier, on time deposits with a bank made on or after July 1, 1995. When a time deposit is renewed retrospectively, the relevant date for deciding the applicability of Section 194A would be that date of renewal. Thus, if the time deposit is renewed after July 1,

1995, the tax deduction at source will have to be made from interest paid or credited in respect of such a time deposit.

(Sd.)
K.G.Bansal
Director(TPL)
[F. No.133/101/95-TPL]

4.4 Circular No.720 of 30th August, 1995
Returns under Section 206 - TDS - Clarification -payment to Advertising co –Whether under Section 194C or 194J
F.No. 142/42/95-TPL

1. It has been brought to the notice of the Board that in some cases persons responsible for deducting tax at source are deducting such tax by applying more than one provision for the same payment. In particular, it has been pointed out that the sums paid for carrying out work of advertising are being subjected to deduction of tax at source under Section 194C as payment for work contract as also under Section 194J as payments of fees for professional services.

2. It is hereby clarified that each Section, regarding TDS under Chapter XVII, deals with a particular kind of payments to the exclusion of all other Sections in this chapter. Thus, payment of any sum shall be liable for deduction of tax only under one Section. Therefore, a payment is liable for tax deduction only under one Section.

(Sd.)
Anirudh Kumar,
Under-Secretary to the
Government of India.
[F.No. 142/42/95-TPL]

4.5 TDS from Payment of rent – Clarification
Circular no.718 of 22nd August 1995
F.No. 275/60/94-IT(B).

Subject: Deduction of tax at source from payment of rent under Section 194-I of the Income-tax Act, 1961-Clarification regarding.

The Finance Act, 1994 introduced Section 194-I in the Income-tax Act, 1961, which provides for deduction of tax at source from payment of income by way of rent. This Section as amended by Finance Act, 1995 reads as follows:

"194-I. Any person, not being an individual or a Hindu undivided family, who is responsible for paying to any person any income by way rent, shall be, at the time of credit of such income to the account of the payee or at the time of payment thereof in cash or by the issue of cheque or draft or by any other mode, whichever is earlier, deduct income-tax thereon at the rate of -

(a) Fifteen per cent if the payee is an individual or a Hindu Undivided Family; and

(b) twenty per cent in other cases;

Provided that no deduction shall be made under this Section where the amount of such income, or as the case may be, the aggregate of the amount of such income credited or paid or likely to be credited or paid during the financial year by the aforesaid person to the account of, or, to the payee, does not exceed one hundred and twenty thousand rupees.

Explanation: For the purposes of this Section -

(i) "rent" means any payment, by whatever name called, under any lease, sub-lease, tenancy or any other agreement or arrangement for the use of any land or any building (including factory building), together with furniture, fittings and the land appurtenant thereto, whether or not such building is owned by the payee,

(ii) where any income is credited to any account, whether called "Suspense Account" or by any other name, in the books of account of the person liable to pay such income, such crediting shall be deemed to be credit of such income to the account of the payee and the provisions of this Section shall apply accordingly."

The Board has received a number of queries from various persons regarding the application of the aforesaid provision. These queries have been carefully considered by the Board and the following clarifications are issued for information and guidance of all concerned:

Query No.1: Whether tax is required to be deducted at source where rent has been paid in advance before 1-6-1994?
Answer: Where an advance of rent has been paid before 1-6-1994, there is no requirement for deduction of tax at source.

Query No.2: Whether tax is required to be deducted at source where a non-refundable deposit has been made by the tenant?
Answer: In cases where the tenant makes a non- refundable deposit tax would have to be deducted at source as such deposit represents the consideration for the use of the land or the building etc., and, therefore, partakes the nature of rent as defined in Section 194-I. If, however, the deposit is refundable, no tax would be deductible at source. It is further clarified that if the deposit carries interest, the tax to be deducted on the amount of interest will be governed by Section 194A of the Income-tax Act.

Query No.3: Whether the tax is to be deducted at source from warehousing charges?

Answer: The term 'rent' as defined in Explanation (i) below Section 194-I means any payment by whatever name called, under any lease, sub-lease, tenancy or any other agreement or arrangement for the use of any building or land. Therefore, the warehousing charges will be subject to deduction of tax under Section 194-I.

Query No.4: On what amount the tax is to be deducted at source if the rentals include municipal tax, ground rent, etc.?

Answer: The basis of tax deduction at source under Section 194-I is "income by way of rent". Rent has been defined, in the Explanation (i) of Section 194-I, to mean any payment under any lease, tenancy, agreement, etc., for the use of any land or building. Thus if the municipal taxes, ground rent, etc., are borne by the tenant, no tax will be deducted on such sum.

Query No.5: Whether Section 194-I is applicable to rent paid for the use of only a part or a portion of any land or building?

Answer: Yes, the definition of the term "any land" or "any building" would include a part or a portion of such land or building.

(Sd.)

Y. P. Vashishat,

Under Secretary to the

Government of India.

[F.No. 275/60/94-IT(B).]

4.6 Rent –Credit for TDS Circular No.5 of 2001

Sub : Credit for tax deducted at source under Section 199 of the Income-tax Act

A number of representations has been received by the Board pointing out the problems being faced by the assessees in getting due credit for tax deducted at source under the provisions of Section 199 of the Income-tax Act, 1961, in respect of tax deducted in terms of Section 194-I of the Act. Such problems in getting due credit for tax deducted at source mainly relate to the following situations :

(a) Tax is deducted at source under the provisions of Section 194-I of the Act on advance rent pertaining to more than one financial year to be adjusted against future rent.

(b) Subsequent to the deduction of tax at source on advance rent pertaining to one or more financial years :

(i) Rent agreement gets terminated/cancelled resulting into refund of balance amount of advance rent to the tenant,

(ii) Rented property is transferred by way of sale, lease, gift, etc. with tenant in occupation or otherwise resulting into refund of balance amount of advance rent to the transferee or the tenant, as the case may be.

2.1. In the situation mentioned at (a) in para above, difficulty in getting due credit for tax deducted arises because the entire amount of advance rent does not accrue to the assessees as income in one financial year since the income from the property is taxed on the basis of annual letting value whereas the tax is deducted at source on the entire amount of advance rent pertaining to more than one financial year. Therefore, credit for entire amount of tax deducted at source is not allowed in terms of Section 199 of the Act because the credit is to be given for the assessment year for which such income is assessable. Thus, the assessees do not get credit for the entire amount of tax deducted at source in the first assessment year, in which part of the advance rent is offered as rental income, on the basis of the certificate furnished under Section 203 of the Act. Further there is a difficulty in claiming the credit in the remaining assessment years to which balance of advance rent relates in the absence of the certificate for tax deducted at source for these years.

2.2. In the situation as at (b) mentioned at para 1, difficulty in getting due credit for tax deducted at source arises because rental income ceases to accrue to the assessees on account of termination/cancellation of rent agreement or transfer of the rented property subsequent to the deduction of tax at source on advance rent pertaining to one or more financial years. The credit is not given in the hands of the assessees in whose names certificate for tax deduction at source stands because there is no relatable rental income and, further credit for tax is not allowed to any person other than the person in whose name certificate for tax deducted at source has been issued. Thus, in such cases, even though tax has been deducted at source and paid to the Government, due credit for such tax deducted is not allowed.

3. The matter has been considered by the Board and it has been decided that credit for tax deducted at source shall be allowed to the assessees on whose behalf such tax has been deducted and to whom certificate for tax deducted at source has been furnished under Section 203 of the Act as under :

(i) In such cases as referred to in (a) above where advance rent is spread over more than one financial year and tax is deducted thereon, credit shall be allowed in the same proportion in which such income is offered from taxation for different assessment years based on the single certificate furnished for tax so deducted on the entire advance rent.

(ii) In respect of the situation as at (b), credit for the entire balance of tax deducted at source, which has not been given credit so far, shall be allowed in the assessment year relevant to the financial year during which the rent agreement gets terminated/cancelled or rented property is transferred and balance of advance rent is refunded to the transferee or the tenant, as the case may be.

[F. No. 275/56/2000-IT (B) - From Central Board of Direct Taxes]

4.7 Hotel Rooms Taken On Regular Basis

Direct Tax Circular No. 5-2002 dated 30th July, 2002

F.No.275/27/2001-IT(B)
Government of India
Ministry of Finance
Department of Revenue
Central Board of Direct Taxes
New Delhi

To,
All Chief Commissioners of Income Tax
And Director Generals of Income Tax.

Tax deduction at source under 194-I of the Income-tax Act, 1961 and Circular No. 715 dated 8.8.1995. Clarification regarding scope of Section 194-I of the IT Act.

Circular No. 715 dated 8.8.1995 has been issued by the Central Board of Direct Taxes to clarify various provisions relating to tax deduction at source under various provision of the Income-tax Act. Question No. 20 at the aforesaid Circular related to applicability of the provisions of Section 194-I of the Income-tax Act in respect of payments made to a hotel for rooms. The relevant question and answer is reproduced below:-

"....Q.No. 20 :- Whether payments made to a hotel for rooms hired during the year would be of the nature of rent?

Ans :- Payments made by persons other than individuals and HUF for hotel accommodation taken on regular basis will be in the nature of rent subject to TDS u/s 194-I (emphasis supplied)."

In this context, doubts have been raised as to what constitutes "hotel accommodation taken on regular basis" for the purpose.

2. The Board have considered the matter. First, it needs to be emphasized that the provisions of Section 194-I do not normally cover any payment for rent made by an individual or HUF except in cases where the total sales, gross receipts or turnover from business and profession carried on by the individual or HUF exceed the monetary limits specified under clause (a) or clause (b) of Section 44 AB. Where an employee or an individual representing a company (like a consultant, auditor, etc) makes a payment for hotel accommodation directly to the hotel as and when he stays there, the question of tax deduction at source would not normally arise (except where he is covered under Section-44AB as mentioned above) since it is the employee or such individual who makes the payment and the company merely reimburses the expenditure.

Furthermore, for purposes of Section 194-I, the meaning of "rent" has also been considered. "Rent" means any payment, by whatever name called, under any lease .... or any other agreement or arrangement for the use of any and ...." (emphasis supplied).

The meaning of "rent" in sec. 194-I is wide in its ambit and scope. For this reason, payment made to hotels for hotel accommodation, whether in the nature of lease or licence agreements are covered, so long as such accommodation has been taken on "regular basis". Where earmarked rooms are (let out for a specified rate and specified period, they would be construed to be accommodation made available on "regular basis".

Similar would be the case, where a room or set of rooms are not earmarked, but the hotel has a legal obligation to provide such types of rooms during the currency of the agreement.

3. However, often, there are instances where corporate employers, four operators and travel agents enter into agreements with hotels with a view to merely fix the room tariffs of hotel rooms for their executives/ guests/ customers. Such agreements, usually entered into for lower tariff rates, are in the nature of rate- contract agreements. A rate-contract, therefore, may be said to be a contract for providing specified types of hotel rooms at pre-determined rates during art agreed period. Where an agreement is merely in the nature of a rate contract, it cannot be said to be accommodation 'taken on regular basis', as there is no obligation on the part of the hotel to provide a room or specified set of rooms. The occupancy in such cases would be occasional or casual. In other words, a rate-contract is different for this reason from other agreements, where rooms are taken on regular basis. Consequently, the provisions of sec. 194-I while applying to hotel accommodation taken on regular basis would not apply to rate contract agreements.

Sd/-
(Anand Jha)
Deputy Secretary to the Govt. of India

4.8 Taxability of export commission payable to non-resident agents Circular No.786 dated 7-2-2000

In the Audit Report for 1997-98 (D P No 79(I.T.) The Comptroller & Auditor General (C&AG) raised an objection that the Assessing Officer in computing the Profits and Gains of Business or Profession, in a case in Mumbai charge, had wrongly allowed a deduction in respect of a payment to a non-resident where tax had not been deducted at source. The nature of the payment in this case was export commission and charges payable for services rendered outside India. In the view of C&AG the expenditure should have been disallowed in accordance with the provisions of Section 40(a)(i) of the Income-tax Act, 1961. It has come to the notice of the Board that a similar view, on the same set of facts has been taken by some Assessing Officers in other charges.
The deduction of tax at source under Section 195 would arise if the payment of commission to the non-resident agent is chargeable to tax in India. In this regard attention to CBDT Circular No 23 dated 23.7.1969 is drawn, where the taxability of 'Foreign Agents of Indian Exporters" was considered along with certain other specific

situations. It had been clarified then that where the non-resident agent operates outside the country, no part of his income arises in India. Further, since the payment is usually remitted directly abroad it cannot be held to have been received by or on behalf of the agent in India. Such payments are therefore held to be not taxable in India. The relevant Sections, namely Section 5(2) and Section 9 of the Income-tax Act, 1961 not having undergone any change in this regard, the clarification in Circular No 23 shall prevails. No tax is therefore deductible under Section 195 and consequently the expenditure on export commission and other related charges payable to a non-resident for services rendered outside India becomes allowable expenditure. On being apprised of this position, the Comptroller & Auditor General have agreed to drop the objection referred to above.

4.9 Procedure for refund of tax deducted at source by the person deducting the tax

Circular No.790 of 20th April, 2000 Section 195
[F. No. 500/92/96 FTD]

1. The Board has issued Circular no. 769, dated 6th August, 1998 [published at (1998) 148 CTR (St) 118), laying down procedure for refund of tax deducted under Section 195, in certain situations to the person deducting the tax at source from the payment to the non-resident. After reconsideration, Circular no. 769 is revoked with immediate effect and refund to the person deducting tax at source under Section 195 shall be allowed in accordance with the provisions of this Circular.

2. The Board had received representations for approving grant of refund to persons deducting tax at source under Section 195 of the Income-tax Act, 1961. The cases referred to the Board mainly related to circumstances where after the deposit into Government account of tax deducted at source under Section 195:

(a) the contract is cancelled and no remittances is made to the non-resident;

(b) the remittance is duly made to the non-resident, but the contract is cancelled, In such cases, the remitted amount may have been returned to the returned to the person responsible for deducting the tax at source.

In the case mentioned above, income does not accrue to the non-resident. The amount deducted as tax under Section 195 and paid to credit of Government therefore belongs to the deductor. At present, a refund is given only on a claim being made by the non-resident with whom the transaction was intended.

3. In the type of cases referred to in sub-paragraph (a) of paragraph 2, the non-resident not having received any payment would not apply for a refund. For cases covered by sub paragraph (b) of paragraph 2, no claim may be made by the non-resident where he has no further dealings with the resident deductor of tax. This resident deductor is,

therefore, put to genuine hardship as he would not be able to recover the amount deducted and deposited as tax.

4. The matter has been considered by the Board. In the type of cases referred to above, where no income has accrued to the non-resident due to cancellation of contract, the amount deposited to the credit of Government under Section 195 cannot be said to be 'tax'. It has been decided that this amount can be refunded, with prior approval of Chief Commissioner concerned to the person who deducted it from the payment to the non-resident under Section 195.

5. The refund being made to the person who made the payment under Section 195, the Assessing Officer may after giving intimation to the deductor, adjust it against any existing tax liability of the deductor, adjust it against any existing tax liability of the deductor under the Income-tax Act, 1961, Wealth-tax Act, 1957 or any other direct tax law. The balance amount , if any, should be refunded to the person who made such payment under Section 195. A separate refund voucher to the extent of such liability under each of the direct taxes should be prepared by the Income-tax Officer or the Assessing Officer in favour of the "Income-tax Department" and sent to the bank along with the challan of the appropriate type. The amount adjusted and the balance, if any, refunded would be debitable under the sub-head "Other refunds" below the minor head "Income-tax on Companies" - major head "020 - Corporation Tax" or below the minor head "Income-tax other than Union Emoluments" major head "021 - Taxes on Incomes other than Corporation Tax" depending upon whether the payment was originally credited to the major head "020 - Corporation Tax" or to the major head "021 - Taxes on Income other than Corporation Tax". Since the adjustment / refund of the amount paid would arise in relation to the deduction of tax at source, the recording of the particulars of adjustment / refund of the amount paid would arise in relation to the deduction of tax at source, the quarterly statement of TDS / annual return under the signature of the Income-tax Officer or the Assessing Officer at the end of the statement, i.e. below the signature of the person furnishing the statement.

6. Refund to the person making payment under Section 195 is being allowed as income does not accrue to the non-resident. The amount paid into the Government account in such cases, is no longer 'tax'. In view of this, no interest under S 244A is admissible on refunds to be granted in accordance with this Circular or on the refunds already granted in accordance with Circular no. 769.

7. A refund in terms of this Circular should be granted only after obtaining an undertaking that no certificate under S. 203 of the Income-tax Act has been issued to the non-resident. In cases where such a certificate has been issued, the person making the refund claim under this Circular should either obtain it or should indemnify the Income-tax Department from any possible loss on account of any separate claim of refund for the same amount by the non-resident.

8. The refund as per this Circular is permitted only in respect of transactions with non-

residents, which have either not materialised or have been cancelled subsequently. It therefore, needs to be ensured by the Assessing Officer that they disallow corresponding transaction amount, if claimed as an expense in the case of person making refund claim.

9. It is hereby clarified that refund shall not be issued to the deductor of tax in the cases referred to in clause (i)(c) of Paragraph 1 of Circular no. 769, dated 6th August, 1998.

10. The limitation for making a claim of refund under this Circular shall be two years from the end of the financial year in which tax is deducted at source.

The contents of this Circular may be brought to the notice of all the Assessing Officers working in your charge.

(Sd.) Rajat Bansal,
Officer on Special Duty (FTD)

4.10 Section 197A of the Income-tax Act read with rule 29C of the Income-tax Rules, 1962- Clarification regarding Form 15G ,15H

Circular No. 351 of 26th November, 1982 TDS - Exemption - Dividends/ Interest

F. No. 142(32)182-TPL.

1. The Finance Act, 1982, has inserted a new Section 197A in the Income-tax Act with effect from 1st June, 1982. The Section enables an individual who is resident in India and whose estimated total income of the previous year is less than the minimum liable to income-tax to receive interest on securities, dividends and other interest without deduction of tax at source under Sections 193, 194 and 194A of the Income-tax Act on furnishing a declaration, in duplicate, in the prescribed form and verified in the prescribed manner. Rule 29C and Form Nos. 15F, 15G and 15H have been inserted in the Income-tax Rules, 1962, by the Income-tax (Fifth Amendment) Rules, 1982, prescribing the forms for the purposes of Section 197A of the Income-tax Act and laying down the procedure for furnishing the declaration form.

2. The facility of claiming payments of interest on securities, dividends, etc. under Section 197A of the Income-tax Act is available only in the case of individuals who are resident in India within the meaning of Section 6 of the Act. Accordingly, it is not permissible for Hindu undivided families and other categories of tax-payers to claim payments of interest on securities, dividends, etc. without deduction of tax at source on furnishing the declaration in Form Nos. 15F, 15G or 15H.

3. The declaration in Form No. 15F, Form No. 15G or, as the case may be, Form No. 15H is to be furnished by the declarant to the person responsible for paying any income of the nature referred to in Section 193 or Section 194 or, as the case may be, Section

194A of the Income-tax Act. As defined in Section 204 of the Income-tax Act, the expression "person responsible for paying" for the purposes of the aforesaid Sections means(a) in the case of payments of income chargeable under the head "Interest on securities" (other than payments made by or on behalf of the Central Government or the Government of a State), the local authority, corporation or company, including the principal officer thereof; and(b) in the case of credit or payment of any other sum chargeable under the Income-tax Act, the payer himself, or, if the payer is a company, the company itself including principal officer thereof.Section 2(35) of the Income-tax Act defines "principal officer" with reference to a local authority, a company, any other public body or any association of persons or body of individuals, to mean-(a) the secretary, treasurer, manager or agent of the authority, company, organization or body; or(b) any person connected with the management or administration of the local authority, company, association or body upon whom the Income-tax Officer has served a notice of his intention of treating him as the principal officer thereof.Hence, in cases where the declaration in Form No. 15F, 15G or 15H is to be furnished for the purposes of receiving any interest on securities (other than any security of the Central Government or a State Government), dividends or interest other than interest on securities, payable by any person other than the Central Government or a State Government the declaration may be furnished to the local authority, corporation, company or the secretary, treasurer, manager or agent of the local authority, corporation or company. For the purposes of obtaining interest on any Government security without deduction of tax at source, the declaration in Form No. 15F may be furnished to the public debt officers and treasury officers who are responsible for paying the interest on such securities.

4. The effect of non obstante clause in Section 197A of the Income-tax Act is that it supersedes the provisions of Sections 193, 194 and 194A of the Act only in so far as these cast a legal obligation on the person responsible for paying the income of the nature referred to in the said Sections to deduct tax at source. Thus, the provisions of Sections 193, 194 and 194A which provide a facility for receiving the income referred to therein without deduction of tax at source continue to be in force and the facility provided in the new Section 197A is in addition to the facility provided under the existing provisions in Sections 193, 194 and 194A of the Income-tax Act.

5. The declaration in Form No. 15F, 15G or 15H as explained above is to be furnished to the person responsible for paying the income which is sought to be received without deduction of tax at source. As the declarant has to state that his estimated total income of the previous year in which the income of the nature referred to in Section 193, 194 or 194A is to be included in computing his total income is below the exemption limit, it will be sufficient if only one declaration is made in respect of the income of each year before each person responsible for making the payment. Hence, where payments are to be made by the same person more than once in a year, the declaration in the relevant form may be furnished before the first payment in a year becomes due. It may also be noted that in the declaration in Form No. 15F, 15G or 15H particulars of only such Securities, shares or as the case may be, other deposits are to be furnished the income from which is payable by the person to whom the declaration is furnished. For

example, in the declaration in Form No. 15G furnished to company "A" it is not necessary for the declarant to give particulars of the shares held by him in other companies.

4.11 Circular No.285 of 21st October, 1980
TDS - Salary - Excess Payment - Refunds

F. No. 275/77/79-IT(B).

1. Deduction of tax at source-Payment in excess of the amount actually deducted or deductible from salaries and other types of payments under Sections 192 to 194D of the Income-tax Act-Refund / Adjustment of.

The Board have been considering the manner of refunding the amount paid in excess of the tax deducted and/or deductible (whichever is more) under Sections 192 to 194D of the Income-tax Act, 1961. The Board are advised that such excess payment can be refunded, independently on the Income-tax Act, to the person responsible for making such payment subject to necessary administrative safeguards.

2. In suppression of the earlier instruction on the subject the following procedure is laid down to regulate the refund of such excess payments.

3. The excess payment would be the difference between the actual payment made by the deductor and the tax deducted at source or that deductible, whichever is more. This amount should be adjusted against the existing tax liability under any of the Direct Tax Acts. After meeting such liability, the balance amount, if any, should be refunded to the assessee.

4. Where the tax is deducted at source and paid by the branch office of the assessee and the quarterly statement/annual return (in case of salaries) of tax deduction at source is filed by the branch, such branch office would be treated as a separate unit independent of the head office. After meeting any existing tax liability of such a branch, which would normally be in relation to the deduction of tax at source, the balance amount may be refunded to the said branch office. The Income-tax Officer, who will refund the amount, would be the one who receives the quarterly statement/annual return (in case of salaries) of tax deduction at source from that branch office and keeps record of the payments of TDS made by that branch.

5. The adjustment of refund against the existing tax liability should be made in accordance with the present procedure on the subject. A separate refund voucher to the present procedure on the subject. A separate refund voucher to the extent of such liability under each of the direct taxes should be prepared by the Income-tax Officer in favour of the "income-tax department" and sent to the bank along with the challan of the appropriate type. The amount adjusted and the balance, if any, refunded would be debatable under the sub-head "Other refunds" below the minor head "Income-tax on companies" - major head "020-Corporation tax" or below the minor head "Income-

tax other than union emoluments" - major head "021-Taxes on Incomes other than Corporation-Tax" according as the payment has originally credited to the major head "020- Corporation Tax" or the major head "021-Taxes on Incomes other than Corporation Tax".

6. Since the adjustment/refund of the amount paid in excess would arise in relation to the deduction of tax at source, the recording of the particulars of adjustment/refund should be done in the quarterly statement of TDS/annual return (in case of salaries) under the signatures of the ITO at the end of the statement, i.e. below the signature of the person furnishing the statement.

4.12 Circulars F. NO. 20/23/67/IT(A-I) DATED 28TH JULY, 1967 Grant of exemption certificates to charitable trusts SECTION 197

A number of cases have come to the notice of the Board, where charitable trusts, whose income is exempt under s. 11, are filing applications for refund every year to claim refund in respect of tax deducted at source under s. 193 or s. 195. The Board desire that in such cases the ITOs should be instructed to bring to the notice of the Trusts, the provisions of s. 197, under which the Trust can ask the ITO to issue a certificate in its favour directing that either no tax should be deducted at source or the deduction should be made at a lower rate. These certificates should be promptly issued by the ITOs so that the Trusts can collect their interest and dividend income without deduction of tax at source. The certificates issued by the ITOs can be reviewed by them once in three years

4.13 CIRCULAR NO. 774 Issue of certificate under Section 197(1) of the Income-tax Act 17thMarch,1999

Section 197(1) of the Act envisages that, where tax is deductible at source in terms of Sections 192, 193, 194, 1994A, 194D, 194-I, 194K and 195 of the Income-tax Act, and the recipient justifies the deduction of tax at any lower rate or no deduction of tax to the satisfaction of the Assessing Officer, the Assessing Officer shall issue an appropriate certificate. It has come to the notice of the Board that in certain charges a practice has developed to issue certificates under Section 197(1) of the Income-tax Act, even after the credit or payment of amounts subject to tax deduction at source. This is not in accordance with the provisions of law.

It is, therefore, clarified that the certificate issued under Section 197(1) of the Income-tax Act will be applicable only in respect of credit or payments, as the case may be, subject to tax deduction at source, made on or after the date of such certificate. Therefore, no certificate under Section 197(1) of the Income-tax Act should be issued after the amounts subject to tax deduction at source stand credited or paid, whichever is earlier.

In other words, henceforth application requesting for certificate under Section 197(1)

should not be acted upon if submitted after credit/payment of the amount subject to tax deduction at source. However, assessees having genuine hardship in submitting such applications on time may refer to the Board for condonation of delay in terms of Section 119(2)(b) of the Income-tax Act.

SOURCE : [F.No. 275/57/98-IT(B)-From Central Board of Direct Taxes

Top of Form

Bottom of Form

5. IMPORTANT JUDGEMENTS

5.1 MITSUI & COMPANY LTD. vs. DEPUTY COMMISSIONER OF INCOME TAX ITAT, DELHI 'C' BENCH, (1999) 65 TTJ (Del) 1

Penalty under s. 271C-Failure to deduct tax at source-Salary paid outside India to expatriate employees–Expatriate employees deputed at project office and liaison office of a non-resident company (assessee) in India–Tax was deducted from salaries paid to them in India but not from retention/continuation pay which was paid abroad–On enquiry from Asstt. CIT, both the offices duly furnished the necessary information and paid the shortfall in TDS with interest in Government account suo motto–Thus, it cannot be said that assessee did not co-operate with the Department-Copies of documents impounded during the course of survey were supplied to assessee–company only on the intervention of High Court–Inspection of penalty records however, not allowed-Revenue has violated the principles of natural justice-Penalty deserves to be quashed on this count alone-Besides, there was reasonable cause for not deducting tax on payments abroad-Based on legal opinion of its internal legal cell, the assessee–company had a bona fide belief that such payment was not taxable in India and the provisions of Chapter XVII-B are not applicable-Penalty under s. 271C not exigible.

5.2 DEPUTY DIRECTOR OF SMALL SAVINGS vs. INCOME TAX OFFICER ITAT, MADRAS 'A' BENCH (2001) 70 TTJ (Mad) 695 : (2000) 75 ITD 152 (Mad)

TDS-Under s. 194B-Penalty under s. 271C-Distribution of prizes under Gift Linked Savings Mobilisation Scheme-Dy. Director of Small Savings conducted draw for distribution of prizes based on gift coupons issued to depositors of specified savings schemes under an incentive scheme of the Government and distributed prizes after the draw–None of the persons who obtained the gift coupons were losers because they became entitled to coupon free of cost when they invested a sum of Rs. 1,000-There was no sale or purchase of chance–There was no risk of loss–Return is more than what was deposited by the depositors-Transaction never assumed the character of either 'raffle' or 'lottery'-Provisions of s. 194B not applicable-Penalty under s. 271C could not be levied for not deducting tax from the prizes-Further, the assessee, Dy. Director of Small Savings, being a functionary and subordinate to Director of Small Savings, cannot be said to be assessee in default for the purpose of s. 201(1A).

5.3 ASSISTANT COMMISSIONER OF INCOME TAX vs. U.P. NATIONAL MFG LTD. ITAT, ALLAHABAD 'A' BENCH (2000) 69 TTJ (All) 503 * Also Asstt. CIT vs. Cinni Ltd. (ITA No.481/All/1994; Asst. yr 1992-93) and Asstt. CIT vs. Tullo Motors (P) Ltd. (ITA No. 482/All/1994; Asst. yr. 1992-93).

Penalty under s. 271C-Failure to deduct tax at source-Reasonable cause-

Assessees who were liable to deduct tax at source under s. 194H moved petitions to CBDT for exemption under s. 194H(2)-It cannot be said that the assessees exercised the right either to thwart the provisions of s. 194H(1) or had mala fide intention-Pending decision of CBDT assessees opted not to deduct and pay tax–Assessees' action can in no way be said to be with an intention to defy the provisions of law–Assessees were neither wrong nor had defined settled law by entertaining a bona fide belief that during pendency of petition before CBDT they were not to comply with provisions of s. 194H(1) –Assessees could entertain belief that they were not liable to deduct tax at source during pendency of their petition and this was a reasonable cause for not deducting and paying tax-Requirements of s. 273B were fully satisfied-Penalty not leviable.

5. 4 INCOME TAX OFFICER vs. TITAGARH STEELS LTD.
ITAT, CALCUTTA 'C' BENCH (2001) 73 TTJ (Cal) 297 : (2001) 79 ITD 532 (Cal)

Penalty under s. 221-vis-a-vis penalty under s. 271C-Short deduction of tax at source-An assessee cannot be punished twice for the same act or omission, by way of two separate penalties which, in nature, belong to the same genus-Penalty proceedings are quasi– criminal proceedings and there is no reason for not applying the underlying principle of Art. 20(2) of the Constitution as also of s. 26 of the General Clauses Act to the penalty proceeding under the IT Act-Provisions of ss. 271C and 221(1) belong to same genus- Therefore, penalties under s. 221(1) as well as under s. 271C cannot be imposed for the same lapse of short–deduction of tax at source-Up to 31st March, 1989, only penalty which could have been imposed, if at all imposable, for the default of short-deduction of tax at source was penalty under s. 221(1) –However, with effect from the said date s. 271C is a specific provision dealing with assessee's failure of non-deduction or short-deduction of tax-General provisions do not override specific provisions–Therefore, to the extent a default is covered by the specific provisions of s. 271C, such default cannot be subject–matter of penalty under s. 221(1) after 1st April, 1989.

5.5 INCOME TAX OFFICER vs. DISHERGARH POWER SUPPLY CO. LTD.
ITAT, CALCUTTA 'B' BENCH (2001) 71 TTJ (Cal) 725

Penalty under s. 271C–Failure to deduct tax at source-Reasonable cause-Penalty under s. 271C is not an automatic consequence of non-deduction or short-deduction of tax at source–Penalty cannot be imposed in case the person concerned can demonstrate that there was a reasonable cause for his failure referred to in s. 271C–When an explanation is offered, it is the duty of the officer to objectively consider the same–Short–deduction of tax at source from dividend occurred due to a programming error in the computer which was programmed to print tax amount up to five figures only and surcharge amount up to four figures only whereas in two cases the figures exceeded these limits and the computer printed wrong amounts–Dy. CIT not justified in rejecting the explanation–There is nothing on record to suggest any mala fide on the part of assessee–Penalty not leviable.

5.6 SENIOR ACCOUNTS OFFICER, THERMAL POWER PROJECT, ANPARA vs. ASSISTANT COMMISSIONER OF INCOME TAX (2000) 66 TTJ (All) 529

Penalty under s. 271C-Failure to deduct tax at source-Reasonable cause-Person responsible for making payment explained that he did not consider the agreement with the payee to be in the nature of a contract agreement requiring deduction of tax at source–Similar payments were made in the past but no default on the part of assessee was pointed out by the Department-Explanation cannot be said to be not bona fide-Thus, failure to deduct tax was not without reasonable cause-Therefore, no penalty is exigible.

5.7 DRILL WELL ASSOCIATES CO-OPERATIVE SOCIETY vs. INCOME TAX OFFICER ITAT, AHMEDABAD 'A' BENCH (2001) 72 TTJ (Ahd) 516 : (2000) 73 ITD 240 (Ahd)

Deduction under s. 80P(2)(a)(vi)–Allowability–Collective disposal of labour of members- Co-operative society formed by some employees of ONGC doing drilling work by engaging 40 to 60 labours not members of the society, is not eligible for deduction under s. 80P(2)(a)(vi)-Certificate under s. 194C exempting a co-operative society from deducting tax at source does not prove the assessee's case for deduction under. 80P(2)(a)(vi)-Conclusive finding as regards eligibility for relief under s. 80P(2)(a)(vi) has to be arrived at in assessment proceedings under s. 143(3).

5.8 KEDIA TAXTILES PVT. LTD. vs. INSPECTING ASSISTANT COMMISSIONER ITAT, CALCUTTA, 'E' BENCH 31 TTJ 401 TDS-

Payment of tax not made-Credit in assessee's hands from whose income, tax was deducted-Credit of TDS and consequently, refund cannot be allowed unless there is evidence in records to show the payment of tax by person deducting the tax-Assessee had not furnished any document which showed the evidence of payment of tax deducted at source-Certificates issued by the parties who deducted the tax at source did not show the date of deposit of tax-In some certificate dates for payment of tax to the credit of the Central Government mentioned but the records do not reveal the payment by the parties concerned-Claim of assessee in respect of refund of tax deducted at source was not therefore sustainable.

5.9 ITAT, JAIPUR BENCH (1995) 53 TTJ (Jp) 161

Refund-Interest under s. 244(1A)-Payability qua TDS-TDS stands at par with advance tax for purposes of interest under s. 244(1A)-It has separate existence only till regular assessment-Assessing Officer was not justified in refusing interest under s. 244(1A) qua TDS on the ground that the same is not an amount paid in pursuance of any order of assessment as contemplated under s. 244(1A).

5.10 INCOME TAX OFFICER vs. ELECON ENGG. CO. LTD.

ITAT, AHMEDABAD 'A' BENCH (1991) 41 TTJ (Ahd) 393

TDS-Credit for TDS-ITO refused to grant credit in asst. yr. 1982-83 on the ground that such tax pertained to earlier year-Also refused to give credit in the earlier years on the ground that claim was not made in such earlier years-Not justified-Credit for tax deducted will have to be allowed–This position stands clarified by Circular No. 5- P, dt. 9th Oct., 1967 and amendment to s. 199 w.e.f. 1st June, 1987 has given statutory recognition thereto–Therefore, directions given by CIT(A) for allowing credit for such TDS in asst. yrs. 1979-80 to 1981-82 after necessary verification is justified Appeal [CIT(A)] – Condonation for delay-On the refusal of the ITO to give credit for tax deducted at source either in the year to which the income pertained or in later year when the certificate was produced, the assessee approached higher authorities-Only when assessee's request was not accepted filed the appeals-These circumstances constitute reasonable cause for the delay-CIT(A) has rightly condoned the delay.

5.11 ALLIS INDIA LTD. vs. INCOME TAX OFFICER ITAT CALCUTTA BENCH 'C' (1988) 24 ITD (CAL) 495

Tax Deducted at source-Claim of credit for tax deducted at source from assessee's income-Person deducting tax not paying same into the account of Central Government–Assessee entitled to deduction of TDS.

Sec. 205 puts bar against direct demand on the assessee which mentions "where tax is deductible at source...the assessee shall not be called upon to pay tax himself to the extent to which tax has been deducted from that income". It is thus abundantly clear from the aforesaid provisions that the assessee from whose income–tax has been deducted at source in accordance with the provisions contained in the Income-tax Act, he is entitled to credit of the said tax irrespective of whether the person deducting the tax has credited the same to the Central Government or not. The person deducting the tax at source is in a sense statutory agent of the Central Government and for his default no assessee can be made to suffer. The words used in s.199 "and paid to the Central Government" in the context means "payable to the Central Government". In this view of the matter the assessee is entitled to deduction of TDS as tax paid.

An assessee is entitled to reduction from tax payable by him of tax deducted at source from payments due to him irrespective of whether the payer has deposited such TDS in the Central Government account or not.

Words and phrases-Word "paid"-Used in s.199-means "payable" to the Central Government.

The words paid to Central Government used in s.199 means "payable" to Central Government.

5.12 G.U.J. JAEGER GMBH vs. INCOME TAX OFFICER ITAT, BOMBAY 'A' BENCH (1991) 39 TTJ (BOM) 231 : 37 ITD 64

Advance tax-Interest under s. 217–Liability for deduction of tax is on income chargeable though it is deducted when it is paid or credited–In this case, however, it was not deducted because it was not paid or credited to assessee's account-In these circumstances assessee could not be charged with interest under s. 217 not because it was not liable to pay advance tax but because there would remain no tax payable by assessee as advance tax if tax deductible at source is taken into consideration.

5.13 PHILIPS INDIA LTD. vs. INCOME TAX OFFICER ITAT, BOMBAY 'D' BENCH (1996) 56 TTJ (Bom) 267 : 59 ITD 390

TDS-Assessee in default-Some of the workmen employed by assessee opted for the Scheme of Voluntary Separation-Compensation paid to them-None of them was employed in managerial or supervisory capacity-No case pointed out where a particular employee did not satisfy the test of s. 10(10B)-Thus while forming the opinion that Rs. 50,000 is deductible under s. 10(10B) in respect of each of the workers who opted for Voluntary Separation Scheme, assessee acted honestly and fairly-Case of assessee falls beyond s. 201.

5.14 INDUSTRIAL FINANCE CORPORATION (I) LTD. vs. INCOME TAX OFFICER ITAT, COCHIN BENCH (2000) 68 TTJ (COCH) 99 : (2000) 72 ITD 449 (COCH)

TDS-Salary-Inclusion of dearness allowance in salary for computing exemption under s.10(13A) of house rent allowance–Where the terms of employment provided for payment of dearness allowance, the ITO (TDS) would be justified in including the same in 'salary' for working out exemption of house rent allowance under s. 10(13A). It can be seen that at the time of the appointment the employees are informed of the terms of their employment and in the terms of the employment, they are informed of the 'pay' and the dearness allowance allowable to them. It is clear that they will draw dearness allowance at the rates prescribed by the Corporation from time-to-time. When the terms of employment provide for payment of dearness allowance, as per the definition of 'salary' in cl. (h) of r. 2 of Part A of the IVth Schedule, salary includes dearness allowance. That means that for the purpose of r. 2A of the IT Rules also salary includes dearness allowance. The contention of the representative of the assessee is that there is no stipulation in the terms of the employment to the effect that dearness allowance would be treated as part of salary. It is not very relevant whether the assessee-corporation treats dearness allowance as part of salary or not. May be that, for the purpose of computing gratuity or other benefits payable to the employees, the assessee takes into account only the basic pay without including dearness allowance. But the Department is guided by the provisions of r. 2A of the IT Rules and cl. (h) or r. 2 of Part A of the IVth Schedule irrespective of the treatment the assessee, as an employer, would like to give to the meaning of the term 'salary'. It is not possible to agree with the representative that the employees of the Corporation are entitled to get dearness allowance, not in terms of their employment. If the assessee's claim in this regard is correct, there is no need to mention the fact about payment of dearness allowance, in the appointment order itself as part of the terms of employment. If the terms of employment provide for payment of dearness allowance, the same is included in the definition of salary in cl. (h) of r. 2 of Part A of the IVth Schedule. The ITO (TDS) was correct in including dearness allowance in the meaning of 'salary' for the purpose of working out the exemption under s. 10(13A) on the house rent allowance.

5.15 INDUSTRIAL CREDIT & INVESTMENT CORPORATION OF INDIA LTD. vs. FOURTH INCOME TAX OFFICER ITAT, BOMBAY 'C' BENCH (1993) 47 TTJ (Bom) 401

Salary-Conveyance allowance-Payment of conveyance allowance to meet expenditure incurred for commuting between residence and office- Is not in the nature of salary as evidenced from CBDT Circular No. 23(LVIII-8) dt. 9th July, 1956–This is further fortified by Expln. to Proviso to s. 16(1) omitted w.e.f. 1st April, 1989, and Expln. to s. 17(2)–Scale of conveyance allowance not also found to be excessive–Therefore, assessee–employer was not obliged to deduct tax at source on conveyance allowance

5.16. ROYAL CALCUTTA TURF CLUB vs. DEPUTY COMMISSIONER OF INCOME TAX ITAT, CALCUTTA 'E' BENCH (2001) 71 TTJ (Cal) 269 : (2001) 76 ITD 237 (Cal)

TDS-Under s. 194BB-Winnings from horse races-Implies net income after deducting the expense incurred for earning the gross income–Tax is required to be deducted only from the net income arising out of horse race to the punter from any particular race after deducting the investments made by the punter in purchasing all the tickets relating to such horse race-This is also accepted by CBDT in its Circular No. 240 dt. 17th May, 1978-The floor limit of Rs. 5,000 is required to be applied to each case of payment-Accordingly, assessee was not at default in allowing the aforesaid deductions from gross winnings while deducting tax at source under s. 194BB-Orders under ss. 201(1) and 201(1A) set aside- Consequently, penalty under s. 271C corresponding to said amounts also deleted.

5.17 GRINDLAYS BANK LTD. vs. INCOME TAX OFFICER I.T.A.T., CALCUTTA 'B' BENCH (1982) 1 ITD (CAL) 1100

Interest under s. 201(1A)-Leviability–Date relevant–In case of interest to non-residents, interest under s. 201(1A) for failure to remit tax deducted at source, has to be computed from the date of actual payment to the non-residents and not from the date of credit to their accounts–The legislature has advisedly and purposefully used the word 'payment' in s. 195 in contrast to 'credit' in other cognate Sections.

5.18 SHRIRAM PISTONS & RINGS LTD. vs. INCOME TAX OFFICER ITAT, DELHI 'A' BENCH (2001) 71 TTJ (Del) 233 : (2000) 73 ITD 30 (Del)

TDS-Assessee in default–Refund of excess deduction by employer-Employer not depositing the whole of tax deducted from one employee on the ground that excess tax was deducted and deposited in case of other employees, is assessee in default–Once the tax is deducted at source from salary, the employer has to deposit it with Government treasury and refund can be granted only to the employee on assessment-The "assessee" in s. 192(3) is the individual employee and not the collective body of employees adjustment either of increasing or decreasing the TDS is to be made with reference to the estimated income of "the assessee" i.e., an employee and not all of them taken together deducting from some and refunding to other. The contention of the employer is that the shortfall /excess can be adjusted on an overall basis i.e., the total deducted for all employees, total liability for all employees and the balance–if shortfall to be recovered and if excess to be refunded. This interpretation is quite illogical as s. 192(3) is not to be read in isolation with the other sub-Sections of s.192. The crucial word used is "the assessee" i.e., the employee in these sub-Sections and one cannot appreciate that when one comes to 192(3) "the assessee" becomes a group of assessee i.e., all the employees taken together. The adjustment either of increasing or decreasing the TDS is to be made with reference to the estimated income of "the assessee" i.e., an employee and not all of them taken together deducting from some and refunding to other. Sec. 192(3) starts with a reference to "the person responsible for making the payment referred to in sub-s. (1) or sub-s. (2) or sub-s. (2A) or sub-s. (2B)" and on harmonious construction the same relates to adjustment in the case of the individual employee and not an adjustment collectively by taking all the employees together.

Coming to another provision now i.e., s. 200 which stipulates that a person deducting TDS on various amounts paid out is obliged by law to deposit the amount so deducted within the period prescribed into Government account. In other words, the amount so deducted cannot be retained by the employer or used in his business as on deduction it becomes the money of the Government and up to the date of its deposit the employer holds it as a custodian on behalf of the Government as is the position of amounts deducted on account of provident fund etc. from the employees. All such statutory deductions are held on behalf of the Government till deposited. Under these circumstances a refund to one employee after collecting TDS from another on estimated salary income is not in order and clearly outside the legal mandate. In the present case, the company after deducting TDS from certain employees did not deposit the same in the Government account as provided by s. 200 but refunded the same to certain other employees in whose cases there had been excess deduction in earlier months. As rightly argued by Revenue the individual employees were required to claim refunds in their own assessments on the excess TDS. A situation apparently has emerged that the company has given TDS certificates to certain employees showing a particular amount deducted at source whereas a part of the same has not gone to the Government account but "refunded" to certain other employees. In the case of the refundees the TDS certificate would show the correct amount after adjusting the refunds although the deduction is more and which is adjusted in the cases of refunders.

In other words, the company has assumed the role of the ITO and granted "refunds" to some of the employees in whose cases there was excess TDS. The action of the CIT(A) in treating the company as an "assessee in default" for the two financial years under appeal is valid.-Oil & Natural Gas Corpn. Ltd. vs. ITO (1998) 60 TTJ (Ahd) 408 distinguished.

5.19 INCOME TAX OFFICER vs. CADILA LABORATORIES PVT. LTD. ITAT, AHMEDABAD 'B' BENCH (1996) 56 TTJ (Ahd) 156

TDS–Interest under s. 201(1A)-Tax deducted from salaries every month and paid to credit of Central Government every month–Shortfall, if any, made good within the financial year–Assessing Officer not justified in dividing the total amount by 12 to arrive at the amount of monthly tax and comparing it with actual tax deposit in each month-Interest under s.201(1A) not leviable.

5.20 KLM ROYAL DUTCH AIRLINES vs. ASSISTANT COMMISSIONER OF INCOME TAX* ITAT, DELHI 'E' BENCH (1998) 62 TTJ (Del) 268 *Also Asstt. CIT vs. KLM Royal Dutch Airlines (ITA Nos. 6357 & 6358/Del/1996; Asst. yrs. 1987-88 to 1992-93).

TDS-Assessee in default-Non-inclusion of conveyance reimbursement in salary-Assessee reimbursing its employees with conveyance expenditure since long-At no point of time Revenue pointed out that the amounts reimbursed come within the ambit of s. 192–Therefore, it was under bona fide belief that this amount did not require tax deduction at source–Further, there is no specific column in Form No. 24 requiring the assessee to indicate reimbursement of such expenditure-No material to indicate that the conduct of assessee is not bona fide-Order under s. 201(1) not justified.

5.21 PENTAGON ENGINEERING PVT. LTD. vs. FIRST INCOME TAX OFFICER ITAT, BOMBAY 'D' BENCH (1983) 17 TTJ (BOM) 130 : 5 ITD 87

TDS-Interest under s. 201(1A)-Levy of interest is mandatory-Fact that appeal is provided against order under s. 201(1A) does not mean that appellate authority can go into reasonableness of cause for delayed payment-Further, interest under s. 201(1A) is levied from the date of actual payment of salaries to the date of payment of taxes into Government treasury-Sec. 192 refers merely to 'payment'–Assessee so long as does not pay salary to employee, is not liable to deduct tax therefrom–Case remanded it. Interest under s. 201(1A)-Nature-Levy of interest is mandatory-Fact that appeal is provided against order under s. 201(1A) does not mean that appellate authority can go into reasonableness of cause for delayed payment-Further, interest under s. 201(1A) is levied from the date of actual payment of salaries to the date of payment of taxes into

Government treasury–Sec. 192 refers merely to 'payment'–Assessee so long as does not pay salary to employee, is not liable to deduct tax there from–Case remanded.–Grindlays Bank Ltd. vs. ITO (1982) 1 ITD 100 (Cal) relied on.

5.22 GULF OIL INDIA LTD. vs. INCOME TAX OFFICER ITAT, MUMBAI 'C' BENCH (2000) 67 TTJ (MUMBAI) 182 : (2000) 75 ITD 172 (MUMBAI)

TDS-Rent under s. 194-I-Hire charges for storage tanks-For applicability of s. 194-I, rent has to be paid for the use of land or building and nothing else-Tanks for storing lubricating oils are neither land nor building hence rental paid for hiring them does not attract s. 194- I-Storage tanks are either 'plant' or simply a civil construction–Land is not taken on lease separately from the tanks-Lubricant does not occupy a tank in the manner occupancy is understood and the storage tank cannot be regarded as building-Orders under ss. 201 and 201(1A) for non-compliance with s. 194-I set aside.

5.23 KAMAT HOTELS (I) LTD. vs. COMMISSIONER OF INCOME TAX ITAT, Mumbai 'd' bench (2001) 73 TTJ (Mumbai) 608 : (2001) 78 ITD 241 (Mumbai)

TDS-Under s. 194-I-Commission/royalty for conducting catering business-Assessee was permitted to run and conduct catering business in the restaurant/ food outlets owned by two companies-Royalty/commission payable to said companies under the agreements at specified percentage of sale proceeds could not be considered as rent even under the extended definition of the word 'rent' in the Expln. (i) below s. 194-I-Very object of the agreements is to permit the assessee to conduct the catering business efficiently-It was only incidental thereto that the assessee was permitted to use the premises–Since the consideration payable by the assessee in the form of royalty/commission was not for the use of the land or building or the furniture and fittings therein but for allowing the assessee to conduct the business, assessee was not liable to deduct tax from the royalty/commission payments made under the agreements and hence, could not be treated as an assessee in default–Assessee is not liable to interest under s. 201(1A).

5.24 ENTERPRISE INTERNATIONAL LTD. vs. INCOME TAX OFFICER ITAT, CALCUTTA 'E' BENCH (2001) 71 TTJ (Cal) 828 : (2001) 77 ITD 189 (Cal)

TDS–Under s. 194-I-Rent-Even advance payment of rent is required to be taken into consideration for the purpose of s. 194-I-However refundable deposits which are clearly in connection with tenancy agreement did not represent advance rent and therefore provisions of s. 194-I were not attracted.

5.25 INSPECTING ASSISTANT COMMISSIONER vs. TATA CHEMICALS LTD. ITAT, MUMBAI 'D' BENCH (1999) 64 TTJ (Mumbai) 26 : 68 ITD 205 *Also Tata Chemicals Ltd. vs. IAC (ITA Nos. 4937 to 4442/Bom/1987; Asst. yrs. 1979- 80 to 1983-84).

TDS-Interest under s. 201(1A) –Failure to deduct and pay tax under s. 194A-There is an absolute obligation on the payer to deduct tax at source barring some exceptions provided in the statute-These exceptions did not apply during the relevant years to payments made to a company–Payer has no option to deduct or not to deduct tax even if the payee incurs a loss-Liability to pay interest under s. 201(1A) starts from the moment the default is committed by not deducting tax at source at the time of payment or after deducting the tax at source but not paying it to the Govt account within prescribed time and continues till tax is actually paid or till the AO assessing the payee determines that no tax is payable by assessee or orders a refund to be given to that payee-assessee-It would be very unfair and unreasonable to construe s. 201(1A) to mean that interest has to be computed from the date when the tax was actually deducted to the date when the tax was actually paid–This would mean that assessee is not liable to interest–Since the assessee did not deduct and pay the tax at all, it was liable to pay interest under s. 201(1A).

5.26 COMMISSIONER OF INCOME TAX vs. RISHIKESH APARTMENTS CO-OPERATIVE HOUSING SOCIETY LTD. HIGH COURT OF GUJARAT (2001) 171 CTR (Guj) 288 : (2002) 253 ITR 310 (Guj) : (2001) 119 TAXMAN 239 (Guj)

TDS-Interest under s. 201(1A)-Chargeability/Computation–Assessee-society did not deduct any amount of tax which it was required to deduct as per the provisions of s.194C-Payee-contractor had, however, paid advance tax as well as tax on self-assessment with respect to the amount received by it from the assessee–society–There is no question of levying any interest on the assessee as the amount which was payable to the Revenue had been duly paid-Therefore, tax paid by the contractor in its own case by way of advance tax and self–assessment tax should be deducted from the gross tax that the assessee should have deducted under s. 194C while computing interest chargeable under s.201(1A) for failure to deduct tax from payment made to contractor.

5.27 COMMISSIONER OF INCOME TAX vs. PREM NATH MOTORS (P) LTD. HIGH COURT OF DELHI (2001) 170 CTR (Del) 424 : (2002) 253 ITR 705 (Del) : (2002) 120 TAXMAN 584 (Del)

TDS-Interest under s. 201(1A)-Failure to deduct tax at source–Levy of interest under s.201(1A) is a compensatory measure for withholding tax which ought to have gone to the exchequer–Levy is mandatory and automatic-Absence of liability for tax does not dilute the default-Assessee had not properly deducted tax at source as required under s. 192 and same had not been deposited with the Government–Levy of interest was justified The levy of interest under s. 201(1A) is of a compensatory measure for withholding tax which ought to have gone to the exchequer. The provision makes it clear that the levy is mandatory. It is true that the use of the expression "shall" is not always determinative of the fact whether a provision is directory or mandatory in nature. But the context in which the expression "shall" is used in s. 201(1A) makes it unambiguously clear that the levy is mandatory.

The purpose of the levy is to claim compensation on the amount which ought to have been deducted and deposited and has not been done. The use of the word "shall" raises a presumption that the particular provision is imperative. But this prima facie inference may be regarded by other considerations such as the object and scope of the enactment and consequences flowing from such construction. Liability to pay interest arises by operation of law, being automatic. Looking at the nature of levy, it is clear that it is compensatory in character and not in the nature of penalty. It is seen that there are several provisions where the legislature has made a distinction between interest payable and penalty imposable. The ultimate liability for tax being not there does not dilute the requirements for the non-compliance of which interest is levied under s. 201(1A). Judged in that background, the levy of interest was justified and the Tribunal was not justified in directing its deletion.-Sainik Motors vs. State of Rajasthan AIR 1961 SC 1480, Karimtharuvi Tea Estate Ltd. vs. State of Kerala (1966) 60 ITR 262 (SC) : TC 38R.479, CST vs. Qureshi Crucible Centre (1993) 89 STC 467 (SC) and Prahlad Rai vs. STO (1992) 84 STC 375 (SC) applied.

5.28 NEW RAJASTHAN TRADING CO. vs. INCOME TAX OFFICER ITAT, JODHPUR BENCH (1999) 65 TTJ (Jd) 708 : (2001) 77 ITD 295 (Jd)

Penalty under s. 272A(2)(c)-Failure to furnish TDS return under s. 206 in time-Applicability of proviso to s. 272A(2)-Assessee deducted the tax and deposited the same with Government which means that was aware of its legal obligations cast upon him vide s. 194/206 r/w r. 37-Thus it cannot be absolved of the default of non-filing of statement under s. 206-Assessee never approached any authority for condoning the delay for not filing the said return-Therefore, provisions of s. 293B cannot be invoked-However, provisions contained in s. 272A(2) are procedural providing for machinery for levying and collecting penalty–Insertion of proviso to s. 272A(2) did not affect the very ingredients of defaults contemplated under s. 206–Therefore, the proviso though inserted w.e.f. 1st Oct., 1991, is applicable to all the cases pending on that date and the amount of penalty should be restricted to the amount of tax deducted at source.

5.29 RAJASTHAN TRIBAL AREA DEVELOPMENT COOPERATIVE FEDERATION LTD. vs. INCOME TAX OFFICER ITAT, JAIPUR BENCH (1998) 60 TTJ (JP) 427

Penalty under s. 272A(2)(c)-Failure to furnish TDS return-No default in deducting tax at source or in depositing the same in Govt. account-Assessee only committed default in furnishing statement of TDS in Form No. 26–Default is purely of a technical or venial nature-Penalty not justified–Hindustan Steel Ltd. vs. State of Orissa (1972) 83 ITR 26 (SC) relied on.

5.30 DISTRICT EXCISE OFFICER vs. INCOME TAX OFFICER ITAT, DELHI 'E' BENCH (2000) 69 TTJ (Del) 312

Penalty under s. 272A(2)(c)–Delay in furnishing TDS return under s. 206C–

Reasonable cause-Assessee collected tax and deposited the same in time–He, however, did not file the half–yearly return in time under bona fide belief that nothing further was to be done–Default committed by assessee was of a venial nature-Penalty not leviable.

5.31 KALAKRITHI vs. INCOME TAX OFFICER & ANR.
HIGH COURT OF MADRAS (2002) 173 CTR (Mad) 523 : (2002) 253 ITR 754 (Mad)

Penalty under s. 272A(2)(c)–Waiver or reduction under s. 273B–Reasonable cause-If the cause shown is such as to explain the delay as a whole and constitutes a good reason for the non-compliance, no penalty would be leviable-However, where the cause shown is such as to explain a part of the delay or the cause shown is only to mitigate the gravity of the non-compliance, such a cause cannot be extrapolated and treated as being a good cause for the whole of the period of the delay in its entirety–Such cause shown by the assessee would justify grant of partial relief-There is no requirement that the power of the CIT must be exercised either wholly in favour of the assessee or wholly against him when a relief is sought by the assessee under s. 273B in respect of a penalty levied under s.272A(2)(c)-Requisite return was filed by the petitioner only after the ITO issued a show- cause notice-Penalty imposed by ITO was reduced by CIT by 50 per cent-CIT not bound to give full relief The words "reasonable cause" in the Section must necessarily have a relation to the failure on the part of the assessee to comply with the requirement of the law which he had failed to comply with. In case of delay in compliance, the cause shown must be for the whole of the period of the delay and not merely for a part thereof. If the cause shown is such as to explain the delay as a whole and constitutes a good reason for the non-compliance, no penalty would be leviable. However, in cases where the cause shown is such as to explain a part of the delay, or the cause shown is only to mitigate the gravity of the non- compliance, such a cause cannot be extrapolated and treated as being a good cause for the whole of the period of the delay in its entirety. All or nothing, the proposition canvassed by the petitioner would be detrimental to assessees themselves if the choice placed before the CIT in all cases were to be that he should set aside all penalties the moment he finds that there is a cause, though not fully satisfactory, but which may be accepted in part which may justify a grant of a partial relief. If the CIT were to be compelled to grant relief in whole even where the cause shown is not such as to explain in full the delay or the gravity of the non-compliance, the CIT would be compelled to reject and deny all relief. A construction which would preserve the exercise of the power in favour of the assessee in circumstances which warrant it is to be preferred to a construction which would result in the likelihood of denial of relief.

5.32 BANSAL BROS. vs. DEPUTY COMMISSIONER OF INCOME TAX
TRIBUNAL DELHI 'B' BENCH (1998) 64 ITD (Del) 129

Penalty under S. 272A(2)(g)-Failure to issue multiple TDS certificate–Assessee instead of issuing certificate of TDS at the time of credit or payment issued a consolidated certificate on the end of the year-As tax deducted at source deposited is treasury in time and parties not suffered any loss on account of non-issue of multiple TDS certificates no penalty can be levied under s. 272A(2)(g).

5.33 EXECUTIVE ENGINEER, M.S.E.B. vs. DEPUTY COMMISSIONER OF INCOME TAX ITO vs. Executive Engg., M.S.E.B.
ITAT, PUNE BENCH (1994) 48 TTJ (Pune) 47 : 48 ITD 414

Penalty under s. 272A(2)(g)-Validity-Office of assessee, Electricity Board, situated in a small town-No deficit in tax deduction at source-Tax deducted also paid in time- Certificates of tax deducted at source, however, issued in old forms instead of new forms under the amended rule-Penalty under s. 272A(2)(g) imposed to the tune of Rs.1,31,70,600 as against total tax deducted at Rs. 1,61,605–Not valid–There is no lack of bona fides on the part of assessee and the breach, if any, is technical or venial–There was also reasonable cause as assessee was not aware of introduction of new form-Penalty cancelled.

5.34 HARSIDDH CONSTRUCTION (P) LTD. vs. DEPUTY COMMISSIONER OF INCOME TAX ITAT, AHMEDABAD 'C' BENCH (2001) 70 TTJ (Ahd) 266

Penalty under s. 272A(2)(g)-Limitation-Show-cause notice by ITO vis-a-vis Dy. CIT-No IT authority below the rank of Dy. Director or Dy. CIT can impose penalty under s.272A(2)(g)–Only the authority competent to impose penalty can initiate the penalty proceedings–ITO was not competent to issue show-cause notice for default falling under s.272A(2)(g) and therefore the proceedings initiated by the said officer was beyond his jurisdiction–Thereafter Dy. CIT issued a fresh show-cause notice on 24th June, 1994–Limitation of six months period would run from the date of notice issued by Dy. CIT- Penalty order passed on 22nd Dec., 1994, was not time-barred.

5.35 COMMISSIONER OF INCOME TAX vs. HARSIDDH CONSTRUCTION (P) LTD.HIGH COURT OF GUJARAT (2000) 159 CTR (Guj) 364 : (2000) 244 ITR 417 (Guj) : (2001) 118 TAXMAN 760 (Guj)

Reference-Question of law-Penalty under s. 272A(2)(g)-Assessee deducted tax at source under s. 194C and deposited it into Government account within the stipulated time–It, however, failed to comply with s. 203 in sending the certificate to the person concerned–No grievance is being made that loss was suffered on account of late despatch of certificate-Tribunal found that certificate was not forwarded to the payee under the bona fide belief that the same could be forwarded at the end of the accounting year–Relying on the decision in Hindustan Steel Ltd. vs. State of Orissa (1972) 83 ITR 26 (SC) : TC 49R.330 and the peculiar facts of the case, Tribunal held that it was a bona fide mistake and cancelled the penalty under s. 272A(2)(g)-Inference is based on facts and no question of law arises.

APPENDICES

Appendix - I

Rates of Tax Deduction at Source (including Surcharge) for Financial Year 2003-2004

Sl. No.	Nature of Payment	Payment to an Individual, HUF, BOI, AOP		Payment to a firm, local authority, Co.-opt.Society.	Payment to a Company	Liability if sum paid in the year exceeds Rs.
		If aggregate payment does not exceed Rs.8,50,000/-	If aggregate payment exceeds Rs.8,50,000/-			
	Payment to Residents				**Domestic**	
1	Salary	As per computation at regular rates of income				
2	Interest	10.00	11.00	10.25	20.50	5,000
3	Winnings from Lottery, Horse Races, any other game	30.00	33.00	30.75	30.75	5,000 (1)
4	Insurance Commission	10.00	11.00	10.25	20.50	5,000
5	Interest on Debentures, Securities	10.00	11.00	10.25	20.50	2,500 (2)
6	Payment to Advertising Contractors	1.00	1.10	1.025	1.025	20, 000 per contract
7	Payment to Contractors	2.00	2.20	2.05	2.05	20, 000 per contract
8	Payment to Sub-contractors	1.00	1.10	1.025	1.025	20, 000 per contract
9	Payment of deposits under National Savings Scheme,1987; &/or repurchase of units by Mutual Funds/UTI	20.00	22.00	20.50		2,500 (3)
10	Commission on Sale of Lottery Tickets	10.00	11.00	10.25	10.25	NIL
11	Commission/Brokerage	5.00	5.50	5.125	5.125	2,500
12	Rent	15.00	16.50	20.50	20.50	120,000
13	Professional/Technical Services' Fees	5.00	5.50	5.125	5.125	20,000
	Payment to Non-Residents		-	-	Non-Domestic	
1	Income from foreign exchange assets to an Indian Citizen	20.00	22.00	20.50	N.A.	
2	Long-term Capital Gains (Sec.115E)	10.00	11.00	10.25		NIL
	Long-term Capital Gains (Sec.115AB)				10.25	NIL
3	Other long-term Capital Gains	20.00	22.00	20.50	20.50	NIL
4	Interest on debts in foreign currency	20.00	22.00	20.50	30.75	NIL
5	Winnings from Lottery, Horse Races, any other game	30.00	33.00	30.75	30.75	5,000 (1)
6	Payment to Non-Resident Sportsmen or Sports Associations	10.00	11.00	10.25	10.25	NIL
7	Payment of deposits under National Savings Scheme,1987; &/or repurchase of units by Mutual Funds/UTI	20.00	22.00	20.50	20.50	2,500 (2)
8	Rent :-					
	- Upto May 31, 2003	20.00	22.00	20.50	20.50	120,000
	- After May 31, 2003	30.00	33.00	30.75	41.00	NIL
9	Commission on Sale of Lottery Tickets	10.00	11.00	10.25	10.25	NIL
10	Interest or dividend on bonds or Global Depository Receipt	10.00	11.00	10.25	10.25	NIL

NOTE:

1 Rs. 2,500/- for winning from 'Horse Race'.

2 Rs. NIL for security.

3 No deduction if amount paid to heirs.

Appendix II

Due dates for deposit of tax, issue of certificates and filing of annual returns(as amended by notification dt.31st July, 2003).

Nature of Income **A. Tax Deduction at source.**	Time of deposit of tax	Time of issue of tax deduction certificate[3]	Returns of tax[1] Form No.	Returns of tax[1] Time Limit
Salary	Within one week from the last date of the month in which deduction is made.	Within one month from the close of the financial year	24	June 30 every year
Interest on securities	Within one week from the last day of the month[2]	Within one month from the end of the month during which credit is made or the amount is paid	25	June 30 every year
			27 (Statement of interest payable to non-resident)	Within 14 days from the end of qurarter.
Interest other than Interest on Securities	-do-	-do-	26	June 30 every year
Dividends	Within one week from the last date of the month in which deduction is made.	-do-	26	By April 30 every year
			27 (Statement of dividend payable to non-resident)	Within 14 days from the end of qurarter.
Winnings from lottery or cross word puzzle	- do-	-do-	26	June 30 every year
Winnings from Horse Race	- do-	-do-	26	June 30 every year
Payment to contractor/ Sub-Contractor	Within one week from the last day of the month.[2]	-do-	26	June 30 every year
Insurance commission	-do-	Within one month from the close of the financial year	26	-do-
Payment to Non-Resident Sportsmen or Sports Associations	-do-	Within one month from the end of the month.	27	Within 14 days from the end of qurarter.
National Savings Scheme	Within one week from the last date of the month in which deduction is made.	-do-	26	June 30 every year
Equity Linked Savings Scheme	- do -	-do-	26	-do-
Commission on Sale of Lottery Tickets	Within one week from the last day of the month.[2]	-do-	26	-do-
Rent	-do-	-do-	26	-do-
Professional/Techinical Services' Fees	-do-	-do-	26	-do-
Income In respect of units	Within one week from the last date of the month in which deduction is made.	-do-	26	June 30 every year
Payment to Non-Resident (Sec. 195, Sec. 196A, Sec.196B)	Within one week from the last day of the month.[2]	-do-	27	Within 14 days from the end of qurarter.
Income from foreign currency bonds [Sec. 196C] and Income of Foreign Institu-tional Investors from securities [Sec. 196D]	-do-	-do-	-do-	-do-
B. Tax Collection at Source.				
Tax collected on sale of scrap liquor, IMFL, Timber etc.	Within one week from the last date of the month.	Within one month from the end of the month.	27E	31st October & 30th April

1. Due date of filing all TDS returns for the Financial year 2002-2003 extended up to 30th November, 2003.
2. May 31 if the amount is credited to the account of the payee on the last day of the accounting year.
3. Where income is credited to the account of payee on the last date of the accounting year, TDS certificate is to be issued within a week after the expiry of two months from the month in which income is credited.
   Where more than one certificate is to issued in a financial year, then at the request of the payee consolidated certificate can be issued within one month from the close of the financial year.

Appendix-III

Tax rates as per Double Taxation Avoidance Agreement with different countries

Sl.No.	Country DTAA Between India and	Date of treaty	Tax on dividend Art.	Rate %	Tax on interest Art.	Rate %	Tax on royalty. Art	Rate %
1.	Australia	25.7.1991	10	15	11	15	12	15 20 10
2.	Austria (vide 251 ITR 97 st)	20.9.2001	10	Nil	11	10	12	10
3.	Bangladesh	27.8.1991	11	10 15	12	10	13	10
4.	Belarus	27.9.1997 w.e.f.17.7.1998	10	10 15	12	10	13	10
5.	Belgium	26.4.1993, 19.1.2001	10	15	11	10 15	12	10
6.	Brazil	26.4.1988	10	15	11	15	12	25 15
7.	Bulgaria	26.5.1994	11	15	12	15	13	15 20
8.	Canada	11.1.1996	10	15 25	11	15	12	15 20 10
9.	China	18.7.1994	10	10	11	10	12	10
10.	Cyprus	13.6.1995	10	10 15	11	10	12	15
11.	Czechoslovakia	27.1.1986 as revised 8.12.1999	10	10	11	10	12	10
12.	Denmark	8.3.1989	11	15 25	12	10 15	13	20
13.	Finland	13.8.1998	10	15 25	11	15	12	30
14.	French Republic	10.7.2000	11	10	12	10	13	10
15	Germany (Federal Republic of Germany)	19.6.1995	10	10	11	10	12	10
16.	Greece	11.2.1965	8	20	9	20	7	30
17.	Hungary	30.10.1986	10	15	11	15	12	30
18.	Indonesia	7.8.1987	10	10 15	11	10	12	15
19.	Israel	29.1.1996	10	10	11	10	12	10
20.	Italy	19.2.1993	11	15 25	12	15	13	20
21.	Japan	29.12.1989 modified on 16.8.2000	10	15	11	10 15	12	20
22.	Kazakstan	9.12.1996	10	10	11	10	12	10
23.	Kenya	12.4.1985	11	15	12	15	13	15
24.	Korea (South)	19.7.1985	11	15 20	12	15 10	13	15
25.	Libyan Arab Jamhiriya	2.3.1981	9	Nil	10	20	11	30 20
26.	Malaysia	25.10.1976	11	Nil	12	20	13	30 20
27.	Malta	28.9.1994	10	10 15	11	10	12	15
28.	Mauritius	24.8.1982	10	5 15	11	20	12	15
29.	Mongolia	22.12.1994	10	15	11	15	12	15
30.	Nepal	18.1.1987	10	10	11	10	12	15

Contd.

				15		15		
31.	The Netherlands	30/7.1998 as modified on 30.8.1999	10	15	10	10	12	20 15
32.	New Zealand	17.10.1986 as modified on 12.1.2000	10	10	11	10	12	10
33.	Norway	31.12.1986 as modified on 21.6.1999	11	10 15 25	12	15	13	30
34.	Oman	2.4.1997	11	10 12.5	12	10	13	15
35.	Philippines	12.2.1996	11	15 20	12	10 15	13	15
36.	Poland	21.6.1989	11	15	12	15	13	22.5
36A.	Portugal	16.6.2000	10	15 10	12	15	14	22.5
37.	Romania	10.3.1987	11	15 20	12	15	14	22.5
38.	Russian Federation	21.8.1998 w.e.f. 11.4.1998	10	10	11	10	12	10
39.	Singapore	24.1.1994	10	10 15	11	10 15	12	15 10
40.	South Africa	4.12.1996	10	10	11	10	12	10
42.	Sri Lanka	27.1.1982	10	15	11	10	12	10
43.	Sweden	24.6.1997	10	10	11	10	12	10
44.	Swiss Confederation	20.12.2000 amended by Press Note dt.7.2.2001	10	10	11	10	12	10
45.	Syria	6.2.1984	11	Nil	12	7.5	13	10
46.	Tanzania	5.9.1979	11	10 15	12	12.5	13	20
47.	Thailand	22.3.1985	10	15 20	11	10 25	12	15
48.	Turkey	31.3.1995	10	15	11	10 15	12	15
49.	Turkmenistan	25.2.1997	10	10	11	10	12	10
50.	United Arab Emirates	29.4.1992 reiterated in circular 734	10	5 15	11	5 12.5	12	10
51.	United Arab Republic	20.2.1969	11	Nil	12	20	13	30
52.	United Kingdom	25.1.1993	11	15	12	15	13	15 20
53	United States of America	12.9.1989	10	15 25	11	10 15	12	15 20
54.	Uzbekistan	29.7.1993	10	15	11	20 Nil	12	15
55.	Vietnam (Socialist Republic of Vietnam)	7.9.1994	10	10	11	10	12	10
56.	Zambia	5.6.1981	10	5 15	11	10	12	10
57	Namibia	8.3.1999	10	11	11	10	12	15
58.	Kyrgyz Republic	7.2.2001	10	10	11	10	12	15
59.	Jordan	8.12.1999	10	10	11	10	12	20
60.	Qatar	7.4.1999 as notified. Dt.8.2.2000	-	10	-	10		15
61.	Trinidad & Tobago	26.10.1999	10	10	11	10	12	10
62.	Government of Ukraine	11.1.2002	10	10	11	10	12	10
63.	Government of Ireland	20.2.2002 as modified on 11.3.2002	10	10	11	10	12	10

undation/APP 672
dt 14/1/08